Getting your
Ducks
in a
Row!

Getting your
Ducks
in a
Row!

Robert F. Hartsook, JD, EdD
Editor

ASR Philanthropic Publishing

Wichita, Kansas

Stevenson Consultants, Inc., Sioux City, Iowa has collaborated on this book by providing selected text.

Additional copies of this book are available from the publisher. Discounts may apply to large-quantity orders.

Address all inquiries to:
>ASR Philanthropic Publishing
P.O. Box 782648
Wichita, Kansas 67278
Telephone: 316.733.7470
Facsimile: 316.733.7103
Web Site: www.ASRpublishing.com
E-Mail: info@ASRpublishing.com

Cover designed by Roger Keating
Printed in the United States of America by Mennonite Press, Newton, Kansas.

ISBN: 0-9663673-4-0

Library of Congress Card Number: 00-111912

Publisher's Cataloging-in-Publication
(Provided by Quality Books, Inc.)

Getting your ducks in a row! / Robert F. Hartsook, editor.
--1st ed.
p. cm.
ISBN: 0-9663673-4-0

1. Fundraising.   I. Hartsook, Robert F.

HV41.2.G48 2001   658.15′224
                          QBI01-200082

Dedication

To Austin, my son and best friend.

Contents

Prioritizing & Managing Your Campaign Prospects

Board Involvement & Qualifications

Campaign Leadership & Organization

Campaign Cultivation & Solicitation

Strategies For Recognition & Appreciation

Public Announcement

Campaign Successes

Acknowledgments

Ducks in a Row has been a long time coming. For years I tossed around ways to produce a great how-to book on campaigns that would not repeat what others had already done so well. I knew that any significant contribution to this fund-raising venue would have to inspire confidence in its readers to move forward with their plans and dreams. To that end, this book utilizes new campaign success stories chronicling small campaigns to very large campaigns, local initiatives to national ventures along with practical, how-to information on the anatomy of campaigns.

Over the years, I have been searching for, as well as encouraging, the writing of how-to strategies from individuals in the business that I admire and respect. In particular, I want to thank Scott Stevenson of Stevenson Consultants, Inc., of Sioux City, Iowa. His monthly publication on major gifts fund raising provides the source for many of the how-to segments of this book. His inspiration for these articles includes speakers and presenters from across the country who are practitioners in the field. Scott's agreement to be a part of this process was critical to our ability to move the project forward.

In addition to Scott's work, we were fortunate to have access to many other authors, including Denise Rhoades, R. Eric Staley, Franci Hart, Lee Kensett, Jean Kresse, Melinda McAfee, Norma Murphy, Susan Schneweis, Robert Swanson, Lynn Hawks and Ron Vine. My thanks goes out to each of them for their generosity in contributing their works.

Thanks also to all the campaign chairs and staff represented in the Campaign Success Stories section. Their willingness to take time to review and discuss the strategies and approaches that made them successful was of critical importance to this effort.

The editing of this collection, to give it a consistent voice, was a major challenge. Denise Rhoades, Melinda McAfee, Tami Druzba, Robert Vierthaler, Rita Weighill and Jennifer Aday were important to this process. Shelly Chinberg, Executive Vice President of the firm who has worked with me for 13 years, provided critical review and suggestions that were absolutely necessary for this book's success.

I offer my sincere appreciation to Susan Sellers of ASR Philanthropic Publishing for coordination of this entire project in a timely and organized manner.

Finally, my son, Austin took a look at a draft of the cover and found errors that had been overlooked previously. Thanks to him, I was not embarrassed.

I hope you use this book effectively in your campaign work. I know it can play an important role.

Bob Hartsook

Introduction:
Base the Future on an
Aggressive Vision

Successful capital campaigns are the result of great visions and strategic plans grounded in reality.

Members of the philanthropic profession possess more potential for accomplishing good than they can imagine.

Regardless of titles or job descriptions, they represent the profession of dream brokers. They help others realize what their resources could accomplish if only those resources were directed toward noble ends.

Fund raisers stand in the unique position of recognizing what respective organizations are now accomplishing and yet dreaming about what could be accomplished if sufficient resources were made available.

The ability to see things as they are and yet to imagine what they could be is critical to long-term fund-raising success. The ability to imagine and then to strategize how dreams can transform to vision and ultimately, to reality, will greatly impact an organization's future.

But dreaming of building a great institution alone misses the point. To build an organization of great accomplishment is to determine what outcomes can be realized through major gift funding. Dream about what it would take to provide the best cancer treatment center in the nation, for instance. Imagine what it would involve to produce the greatest number of Fortune 500 CEOs who just happen to be graduates of a particular institution. Consider what it would require to attract the most talented musicians in the world to a specific symphony.

Use the fund-raising position to dream immeasurable dreams. Then share that enthusiasm with those who can turn dreams into reality.

Fund raising affords an organization the opportunity to accomplish untold good. Achievements are just waiting to happen.

Now is the time to begin.

Campaign
Readiness

1

Getting Ready

The best way to make improvements is to assess honestly strengths and weaknesses and then make adjustments that will enhance the strengths and diminish the weaknesses.

A similar approach should be used in evaluating the effectiveness of a development operation. It is referred to as a development audit and serves as a valuable process in improving both short- and long-term fund-raising success.

Many organizations employ the services of a consultant to perform a development audit. Others conduct regular self-audits. Each method has both pros and cons.

Whether an organization is hiring outside counsel or conducting an in-house development audit, here is a check list of systems, programs, and structures that should be analyzed to determine the effectiveness of the overall fund-raising operation:

- **Qualifications of existing personnel.** What are the strengths and weaknesses of each member of the development team? Who has experience with campaigns? Who needs additional exposure to the basics of planned gifts? Identifying individuals' strengths and weaknesses is the first step in advancing the proficiency of the team.

- **Review of job descriptions and organizational structure.** Does everyone have a job description? Have the job descriptions been

3

updated to conform to the current responsibilities of each member of the team? In addition, who reports to whom? Is there a better way of structuring the operation for effectiveness?

- **Budget review.** Are existing resources there to maximize the fundraising performance? Are there adequate resources to generate new and increased gifts? This is where a consultant can oftentimes be very effective in pointing out the need for additional development dollars and additional personnel.

- **Gift history.** It is important to have a clear history of gift support as well as sources of support. How much has been raised on an annual basis? Were the funds restricted or unrestricted? How diversified is the funding base and how much did each constituency contribute? What were the largest gifts?

- **Adequacy of support systems.** How are files organized for maximum effectiveness? Are computer capabilities sufficient? How are gifts processed, tracked, and acknowledged?

- **System of prospect identification, research, cultivation, solicitation, and stewardship.** How are prospects tracked? What methods of prospect research are being utilized? Who is managing the major gift prospect pool, and how is it being managed? How many prospects exist? How many past donors are there, and at what levels have they contributed?

- **Board strength and involvement.** What is the current makeup of the board? To what degree are board members involved, and how much do they contribute annually? Is it a hands-on or rubber stamp board? To what degree have board members been trained?

- **Volunteer strength and involvement.** How many volunteers are involved with the organization and in what ways and to what degree are they structured? How significant is their current involvement in the life of the organization? Are they fully trained for their jobs?

- **Campaign preparedness.** When was the last campaign? How much was raised? How many contributors gave at which levels? How were the funds used? What was the role of the board and volunteers in the effort?

- **Communications analysis.** What printed materials exist that support the development effort? How often is direct mail utilized throughout the course of a year? What does each appeal consist of, and how effective has it been? Have all team members been adequately trained in making presentations and solicitation calls?

- **Media and public relations.** How frequently do news releases appear and in which papers? Does the organization have a clear set of identity guidelines? Is the agency's presence clearly felt by the community or region? What partnerships exist between the organization and the community?

- **Operational plan analysis.** There should be a written plan detailing development plans for the year. Does the plan provide quantifiable goals and objectives with strategies on how to achieve each objective? Does it include an action plan and schedule of activities and events to take place?

- **Strategic plan analysis.** Does the organization have a long-range plan that addresses fund-raising needs over a period of five years or more? How does it complement ongoing fund-raising efforts? Does it include plans to generate endowment gifts?

- **Planned gifts review.** Does the agency have an active planned gifts program in place? Has the board adopted a planned gifts policy, and are members fully supportive of the planned gifts program? Does the program include quantifiable goals and objectives as part of the overall operational plan? How many prospects exist? How many expectancies are there, and what is the estimated amount in planned gift expectancies? How are prospects identified and cultivated?

2

Pre-Campaign Plan with Donors in Mind

Are current fund-raising efforts "donor-driven" or "needs-driven"? Does the campaign take into account the interests of the donor, or simply identify organizational needs and expect donors to find them equally compelling?

The successful campaign will no doubt be balanced between the two.

Peyton Helm, vice president for development and alumni relations at Colby College, stresses the importance of pre-campaign planning and the process of involving both prospective donors and staff in the planning process.

According to Helm, successful strategic planning can take longer than a year and should result in a "campaign inventory" aimed at providing institutional solutions that can be realized with the help of major contributors.

Helm has developed the major gifts grid to link institutional needs with donors' interests. The fully developed major gifts grid is incorporated as part of the institution's case statement.

The grid includes a range of gift levels and corresponding categories of gift types: people, programs, and facilities.

The completed grid is the culmination of strategic planning that links institutional needs with gift opportunities.

The Major Gifts Grid
Strategic Planning

Gift Level	People	Programs	Facilities
$ 25,000	Named Scholarship	Visiting Scholar	Faculty Laboratory
$ 50,000	Named Fellowship	Curriculum Development Fund	Seminar Room
$ 100,000	Faculty Research Fund	Library Acquisition Fund	Auditorium
$ 500,000	Junior Faculty Chair Fellow	Visiting Distinguished	Art & Music Library
$1,000,000	Endowed Chair	Biology Venture Fund	Recital Hall

3

Ready or Not?

Just as it is possible to rate and screen major gift prospects, it is also possible to measure an organization's preparedness for a major campaign.

Those who have been involved with campaigns previously know a successful fund-raising effort involves a great deal of planning time and preparation—in some cases, years.

Whether employed by a seasoned professional or a newcomer to development, the Campaign Preparedness Scale can provide one valuable measurement of an organization's readiness in launching a campaign.

The scale takes into account several factors that represent necessary ingredients for a successful campaign and assigns a weight to each of them. Their sum provides one way of analyzing an organization's ability to pursue major campaign gifts.

Following are the factors included in the Campaign Preparedness Scale and brief descriptions of each:

- **Organization's age.** The longer the agency has been in existence, the better the odds of successfully implementing a major gift campaign. An organization's age reflects the time it has had to gain visibility and build a supportive constituency.

- **Percent of repeat contributions.** Assuming there is a well-established mailing list, what percentage of those on this list contribute on an annual basis? If less than 25 percent contribute, for instance, there may be an inadequate pool of campaign prospects. Remember, past donors are among the best prospects for a campaign.

- **Years since last campaign ended.** Has a campaign just been completed, or has it been years since the institution embarked on a major fund-raising effort? This is an important factor in determining an organization's preparedness for a campaign.

- **Board affluence potential.** Boards of directors play a pivotal role in a campaign's success or failure. In many campaigns, it is not uncommon for current and past board members' gifts to account for as much as 30 to 50 percent of the goal.

- **Board preparedness.** Board members can be affluent, but if they are not motivated to "give and get," they will do little to improve the campaign's success. Judge the board's motivation to invest both time and resources. Also, factor in members' collective track record in soliciting major gifts.

- **Income bracket of top campaign prospects.** Take a long hard look at those who are most capable of making major gifts to the organization. Can the top prospects afford to make $10,000 or $500,000 commitments?

- **Staff preparedness.** A self-audit of the development department will reflect an ability to plan and implement a campaign successfully. Many times, consultants are employed to conduct such audits. How many in the development department have previously been involved with successful campaigns? Are systems in place that allow for the identification, research, cultivation and eventual solicitation of campaign prospects? Are records computerized?

- **Strategic planning.** How much planning has gone into creating the vision that necessitates a campaign? Was this planning "donor driven" or "needs driven"? Have board members and prospects been involved in developing a written plan for the organization's future?

- **Number of donor constituencies.** Do donors represent a narrow base of support, or do they represent a wide range of constituencies (e.g. former clients, community residents, churches, foundations, businesses, organizations, etc.)?

- **Organization visibility.** How aware is the community, state or region of the agency and its role? Is the organization regarded highly by many or a few? Do those with financial resources value the organization?

- **Donor/prospect involvement.** What percentage of the constituency is involved or engaged in the organization's life? The more involved donors are, the more likely they are to support the effort.

- **Time window.** Attempt to measure the climate for the proposed campaign. Is the economy robust, or are businesses cutting back? Are there many other campaigns taking place that would interfere with this effort? How is the competition viewed?

After rating the criteria on the chart that follows, multiply them by their respective weights and add them. Establish a score somewhere between a low of 23 and a high of 115.

Although this campaign preparedness scale is meant to provide only one measurement of a nonprofit's campaign preparedness, a score of 23 to 39 would indicate that more time and preparation are needed before pursuing a campaign, while a score of 40 to 69 would indicate a more favorable potential for initiating a major gift effort. An honest appraisal that results in a score of 70 or more would tend to indicate the time is right to pursue a campaign.

Campaign Preparedness Scale

Criteria	Points	Range	Score (1-5)	X Weight	= Total
Organization's Age	1 3 5	1-5 Years 5-10 Years More Than 10 Years		1	
Percent of Repeat Contributions	1 3 5	Less Than 25% 25-50% More Than 50%		2	
Years Since Last Campaign Ended	1 3 5	Less Than 3 Years 3-5 Years 6 Years or More		3	
Board Affluence Potential	1 3 5	Less Than 30% of Goal 30-50% of Goal More Than 50% of Goal		3	
Board Preparedness	1 3 5	No Fund Development Experience Less Than 20% Have Experience 20% or More Have Experience		1	
Income Bracket of Top Campaign Prospects	1 3 5	Less Than $100,000 $100,000-$200,000 More Than $200,000		3	
Staff Preparedness	1 3 5	Little Preparation Somewhat Prepared Highly Prepared		2	
Strategic Planning	1 3 5	Little Planning Informal Planning Written Plans		2	
Number of Donor Constituencies	1 3 5	1-2 3-5 More Than 5		1	
Organization Visibility	1 3 5	Little Visibility Somewhat Visible Highly Visible		2	
Donor/Prospect Involvement	1 3 5	Under 20% 20-50% More Than 50%		1	
Time Window	1 2 3	Undesirable Acceptable Very Appropriate		2	
				TOTAL	

A Score of: 23-39 means you are not yet ready to initiate a major gift campaign.
40-69 means the timing is more favorable to begin a campaign.
70 or more means go for it!

4

Plan Ahead

Before getting into the actual solicitation of lead campaign gifts, there are a number of important preparatory steps. Two of the most important ingredients for a successful campaign include a committed and financially capable board, and an identified constituency of major gift prospects.

Ask around. Most campaigns fail due to a lack of planning up front. Whether campaigns are a way of life or a new challenge to a nonprofit, it is wise to ask some pointed questions up front, and, prior to a campaign assessment, to determine the organization's preparedness for a campaign.

Direct answers to these questions will help to determine campaign readiness:

- **"How genuine are our campaign needs?"**
  Maybe a new parking ramp seems necessary, but how willing is the constituency to support such an effort? It is vital that fulfillment of campaign needs takes into account their "fundability." In other words, is it the kind of project that donors would find appealing to the point of contributing major gifts? Will completion of the project make a noticeable difference in the nonprofit's ability to fulfill its mission? Will those served notice a difference and be better served?

- **"Do we have a constituency base that is able and willing to respond to those needs?"**
  Has the organization undertaken a campaign in recent years? If so, who were the major donors? These past contributors will be the most likely supporters for a new campaign. If there has not been a major campaign recently, it is important to evaluate the current donors' giving history. How many gifts have been received at various levels on an annual basis? Rate existing prospects. How large is the mailing list, and how familiar is the community or constituency with the organization?

- **"Do we have the resources needed to adequately carry out campaign objectives?"**
  If the constituency is scattered geographically, are there available resources to make personal visits to prospects? Are there sufficient numbers of staff? What about computer hardware and software—is it adequate to accommodate the requirements of the campaign? It sometimes pays to consider a "campaign audit" conducted by a consultant to determine the internal preparedness for a campaign. An "outsider" can often convince the CEO of development needs (i.e., additional fund-raising personnel, upgraded equipment, etc.), that otherwise never seem to get funded.

- **"How committed is our board to achieving campaign success?"**
  It is not uncommon for board gifts to account for as much as 30 to 60 percent of the campaign goal. Board members need to be more than convinced of the need for a campaign. They need to make commitments that will set the pace for gifts that follow. Board members also need to be willing to identify and solicit other major gifts if the campaign is to be successful.

- **"How competent and prepared is our staff?"**
  Who among the fund-raising staff has previously been involved with a campaign? Those nonprofits with little or no background in campaigns would be wise to consider a consultant both in the preparation and throughout the duration of the campaign. Once again, a "campaign audit" conducted by outside counsel will help to determine staff competency and the potential need for additional staff.

If these questions have been fully addressed, and the organization is still prepared to initiate a campaign, a "campaign assessment" will help determine a realistic, yet challenging goal, as well as the campaign format and its duration.

14

Identify Major Gift Prospects Early On

One fact always holds true in major gift fund raising: an organization can only get money from people who have it to give. The more people associated with the organization who have financial resources, the better the chances will be of successfully soliciting and closing major gifts. Building relationships with people of affluence and influence should be your top priority.

5

Campaign Assessment is a Pre-Campaign Must

The decision to pursue a campaign should be based on an organization's: 1) genuine and fundable needs; 2) adequate and capable donor constituency; 3) adequate resources to implement and carry out a campaign; 4) convinced and committed board members; and 5) a competent and prepared staff. This is a necessary first step in the pre-campaign process. After determining that a campaign is justifiable, it is time to pursue the second pre-campaign phase—the campaign assessment.

Although the methods of conducting studies may vary among nonprofits, as well as among consultants, their intentions are quite similar. For the most part, campaign assessments or feasability studies involve a series of questions directed to both past donors and potential contributors in an effort to better understand their perceptions of an organization and to determine the likelihood and possible degree of involvement in a campaign. The completion of a study will help answer the following questions:

1. **Does the cause have validity and appeal?** The answer to this question will demonstrate the donor's perceptions of the organization and should provide some insight into the personal interests of the donor. This information will be helpful in tailoring a proposal for a specific portion of the campaign.

2. **How much can be raised?** Although the study is not intended to serve as a solicitation for campaign pledges, questions can be

17

worded to determine the prospect's willingness to participate as well as what anticipated range of giving the prospect may consider contributing over a specified period of time. Although there is no specified number of prospects to be interviewed during the study, it makes sense to involve as many top prospects as possible. As much as 80 percent of the campaign goal will come from as few as 20 percent of the donor constituency. In fact, many of today's major campaigns result in even greater amounts coming from an even smaller percentage of the constituency.

3. **How long will it take, and how much will it cost?** The answer to this question will not only help determine how much can be raised, but also how long it might take. A consultant can be particularly helpful recommending: 1) a campaign goal, 2) whether the campaign should be incorporated with or separate from the annual campaign, 3) what kinds of gifts should count toward the goal (planned gifts, real or personal property, cash only), 4) the scale of gifts required to achieve the goal, and 5) the readiness of the organization to launch a campaign.

4. **Is there adequate board and volunteer leadership to get the job done?** Board members and key volunteers should be a part of the questioning. If board members' pledges are to be a key part of the campaign goal, their commitment should be obvious. Likewise, successful completion of the campaign will take a great deal of volunteer time. The study will help identify levels of volunteer commitment.

    Completion of the study will strengthen the case for support using comments received throughout the study. It will also be useful in cultivating the interest of top donors, help reveal the competition for funds in the community (or region), and serve to measure how the case stacks up. Finally, the study demonstrates that the organization is serious about improved funding. It also shows what top prospects think of the organization.

The successful completion of a campaign assessment will result in a recommendation to the full board regarding a realistic and yet challenging goal, the intended use of funds to be raised, and the format of the campaign.

6

Use Consultants Effectively

You've made the decision to retain fund-raising counsel. You selected three or four firms to interview with a committee comprised of various representatives from your agency. Now you need to bring some type of analysis to the presentations that have been made.

We recommend an evaluation tool that allows committee members to express themselves on 10 important issues regarding the consultant's ability to facilitate your needs. The form begins with the firm's name and the name of the committee member completing the application.

The introduction reads:

"Please rate your understanding of the philanthropic counsel's fund-raising potential on the following topics utilizing a grading scale of one to five with one as excellent, two as good, three as average, four as fair, and five as poor."

1. **General Philosophy of Fund Raising**
   Rating: 1   2   3   4   5
   How well have the fund-raising counsel's representatives expressed their philosophy of fund raising? How well do you believe that philosophy matches your agency's needs?

2. **Approach to Fund Raising**
   Rating: 1   2   3   4   5
   How would you expect this counsel's representatives to utilize their implementation strategies for a campaign?

3. **Marketing Strategy and Materials**
    Rating: 1   2   3   4   5
    How well will this fund-raising counsel implement aspects of the campaign that must be reduced to writing and be published in some format, or demonstrated in video or on tape?

4. **Campaign Experience with Similar Clients**
    Rating: 1   2   3   4   5
    Does this counsel have experience with other clients similar in size and mission to your agency, and can the counsel demonstrate positive results?

5. **Staffing**
    Rating: 1   2   3   4   5
    Who will be the fund-raising counsel's personnel working with you? How will they assist your agency in implementing, tracking and reporting on all elements of the campaign?

6. **Organization and Structure**
    Rating: 1   2   3   4   5
    Has the organization of the campaign been a good match for your organization?

7. **Training and Education**
    Rating: 1   2   3   4   5
    Can this counsel teach your agency's fund-raising staff how to be successful in the fund-raising solicitation strategy?

8. **Overall Responsiveness and Accessibility**
    Rating: 1   2   3   4   5
    Do we believe this fund-raising counsel's representatives will be there when needed and available at all times?

9. **Overall Commitment**
    Rating: 1   2   3   4   5
    Will they lead your agency appropriately? Will they understand the needs and respond as necessary?

10. **Overall Pressure**
    Rating: 1   2   3   4   5
    This is an important decision for your agency. Will this fund-raising counsel represent you appropriately and meet your needs for the future?

The Right Chemistry

Remember, this evaluation is an attempt to take something that is not qualifiable and try to apply some type of qualifiable strategy. It is only a tool and is not meant to be the definitive document.

If you end up with two or more counsels that rate very closely from a numerical point of view, consider these tactics: Either bring those two counsels in for additional interviewing, or set the evaluation scale aside and decide which counsel you believe has the best "chemistry" with your group on the basis of the strategy.

It is important that everyone on the committee be allowed input. In addition, those individuals who are identified as potential good prospects for major giving to the campaign may well have an appropriate weighted view toward a particular counsel. You would be advised to listen to that view, and key on that advantage.

Your agency's satisfaction level with its fund-raising counsel should be high if you employ this simple formula for the selection process.

When employing a fund-raising consultant, it is important to establish a clear understanding of expectations early on in communications. Points such as starting date, completion date, an overview of the consultant's and client's roles and responsibilities, fee structure, expense allowance, and payment and cancellation terms should be spelled out in a contract or letter of agreement.

Additional details also may be included in the contract: who from the consulting firm will provide the service; where will research and other records will be kept; and will you include language concerning a penalty clause. Also, include reporting protocol and specifics on how and when some job duties should be implemented. These details will depend on the type of project and consulting need(s) in question.

Not covered in the agreement is the essence of a consulting arrangement. It is important to negotiate these nuances as though they were the terms of employment for a new staff member. Each consulting relationship will vary according to the task to be accomplished. As with any other type of employee, setting measurable objectives at the beginning of the relationship will give both a clear understanding of expectations and a way to gauge the long-term effectiveness and potential of consultants.

21

7

10 Impediments to Campaigns

Many of the same issues that existed in fund raising more than a quarter of a century ago remain current-day challenges to the process.

Every fund raiser, at one time or another, has been subject to the "power to excuse." If it were easy to conquer these challenges, they would have disappeared a long time ago.

The following are 10 of the most common impediments to campaigns:

1. **"This is a lot of work."** The tendency is to rely on existing revenue streams: sometimes government or foundation funding that has been ongoing, sometimes annual giving programs, and sometimes earned revenues. If the sources of income have sustained an organization "well enough" over time, the effort necessary to mount a major gifts effort, such as a campaign, may seem exhausting just to consider. The benefits accrued from a successful campaign are difficult to keep in sight when the workload seems so overwhelming. Unfortunately, by the time necessity moves a board or staff to consider a major fund drive, the organization frequently has lost some of its strength to mount the drive. Launching a campaign from a weaker profile compounds the workload far more than would be necessary if launched from a position of strength. Do not expect it to be easy.

2. **"Someone else will do it."** Who, exactly? This comment often comes from board members who may be suffering from the "it's a lot of work" syndrome, or worse, from a lack of commitment to the organization. Proponents of "someone else will do it" are often dodging personal responsibility, and the excuse is a sure sign that some major reorganization or training needs to take place. Also, a version of this excuse may come from among faculty members who like to delineate roles very carefully. These faculty members may also believe admissions and community relations are entirely the responsibilities of others. Campaigns are collective by nature: they succeed to the extent that they attract the support of broad participation. If not currently in a campaign, an organization must always be in a preparatory phase during which an inner circle of friends are informed and involved.

3. **"Don't call us. We'll call you."** This impediment may involve many others on the list, but it has its own ranking because it goes beyond the issue of dollars. The best fund raising is relationship building. In fact, the success of a campaign is in part measured by how well fund raising continues after the campaign. Over and over again, prospective donors give below their capacity (or not at all) because they were not sufficiently informed and involved in the vision of the organization, or, after having given in the past, they now feel forgotten. The fund-raising profession is in part to blame for this—raising funds under strict timetables, meeting goals by deadline, and then moving on to the next job due to success. It is important always to remember the value of relationships. Written stewardship policies and constant reminders in the art of cultivation are necessary—often coming in the form of training. Most importantly, however, new prospects are needed, and that requires work at "friend" raising by sharing the mission before and after soliciting financial support.

4. **"Wham-bam!"** Work hard to guard against the wham-bam campaign. There are firms and fund-raising professionals who seem to specialize in them. Usually such campaigns work by coercion. Leadership is brought on quickly and assigned prospects to solicit with a tit-for-tat mentality. The campaign may be financially successful, but the organization's ability to attract future philanthropy is limited. Donors have given until it hurts, rather than until it felt good, and too often a poor image is left in a community which negatively impacts all campaigns. Wham-bam campaigns have no regard for relationship building, and the dollars are an end, rather

than the means to an end. It is easy to understand why the fund raiser's image as a professional is tarnished sometimes.

5. **"Who's in charge, here?"** On one hand, the challenge to leadership in a campaign is a large philosophical issue that can be, and has been, written about at length. Another more mundane, but extremely important, aspect of leadership is shared ownership. So many vibrant nonprofits, including colleges and universities, are vibrant because of their leaders—particularly the CEOs. Who can fault the success of an organization based on the personal energy of its leader and, sometimes, founder? Nevertheless, the reluctance of leadership to share ownership of the vision of an organization and its programs—even to the point of collaborating with another nonprofit organization, can be a tremendous impediment to a campaign. As funding requests increase, funding partners often talk about the need for collaboration, but only recently have they become militant about enforcing this through their giving. Leveraged giving is aided by collaborative efforts, and shared ownership usually elevates all charitable and educational efforts rather than diminishing them. Egos can stay intact, even in a community effort.

6. **"Experience, anyone?"** Most fund raisers probably believe that the college down the street or the nonprofit next door is far beyond them in fund-raising expertise and campaign experience. Normally, this is more myth than reality. Tremendous ability exists to conduct direct mail campaigns, phone-a-thon solicitations, and special event fund-raisers, but the major gift experience necessary for large, integrated campaigns is rarer than one might think. Most organizations learn as they go without the benefit of major gift expertise. Fund-raising professionals with practiced major gift experience and success are too few to go around, and they are usually the prized acquisition of large university development operations. Consequently, one of the most important roles good counsel plays is the role of major gift training partner who introduces clients to the art of one-on-one cultivation, solicitation, and recognition. This is an impediment to campaigns that can be easily overcome.

7. **"It'll never work."** This is another cry for help. Do the fund raisers and the board really believe in the impact and importance of the organization's mission? If not, they should move on. If they do believe, then the campaign will work. The question usually is not whether or not a campaign can be mounted, but rather, how much

can be raised over what period of time, and through what structure. Any organization with some history and a strong cause has a constituency. Under these circumstances, a case for support can be made. "It'll never work" is sometimes just another version of "it's a lot of work."

8. **"We need it now!"** Impatience sometimes leads an organization into a wham-bam campaign, and often discourages a campaign altogether. The patience to undertake a campaign is linked to long-term commitment and staying power, and these characteristics usually are linked to a belief in what you are doing. A campaign does require stability among its leadership, both staff and board, and the stability often comes because of the proof of program impact on the community. The same words and values keep resurfacing, and impatience can be overcome through a personal and/or collective re-evaluation of the organization's mission. The time necessary to conduct a truly successful campaign—one which ratchets up the organization's ability to do everything better—is well worth the investment. With such commitment, a campaign is over before you know it.

9. **"Filthy lucre."** Philanthropy is sometimes considered just a fancy word for robbery of program funds for administrative gain. But in the best collegiate settings, for example, this is not true. The "filthy lucre terminology" usually comes from a naysayer. The language is often tamed down, and the word of choice becomes "begging." This viewpoint may not be changed entirely. At the same time, however, this misunderstanding of philanthropy or suspicion of the work will become an impediment to a campaign. The true nature of philanthropy and the important mission of the organization must always be held up as noble goals.

10. **"We deserve it."** Jealousy is an insidious impediment to a campaign. In part, because, although it may not stop the mounting of a major fund drive, it can readily cause its failure. The jealousy issue usually manifests in the form of "we deserve it" or "we deserve it more." A well-published opinion piece was written by a dean of a small college on what his college could have done had the donor of an equally well-publicized mega-gift to a mega-university had the wisdom to make the gift to his school. More recently, a $10-million lead gift for a basketball arena met with a huge outcry from faculty and community people who thought the gift could be used better elsewhere (the gift was withdrawn). Jealousy, especially when it concerns contributed money, is indeed an ugly

green monster. Volunteers and leadership infected with jealousy will not cultivate prospects well nor be successful at soliciting support because they have forgotten the importance of their own mission through an obsession with another's.

This list is not exhaustive. Human nature could supply many more impediments, even if these were eradicated. But after decades of dealing with the same demons, some new impediments might be rather refreshing!

Developing Your Case Statement

8

Thinking Big

$\mathbf{T}$hinking "big" involves risk. Thinking "small" is safe. Has the organization created a strategic plan (or vision) that takes small, safe steps, or has it crafted a plan that will clearly distinguish it from other institutions?

To attract the attention of major gift prospects, it is important to develop a strategic plan that is not only comprehensive and well thought out, but that also demonstrates the organization's intent to make major achievements.

To think big and involve prospects in planning a big future, follow this process:

- **Develop the skeleton of a strategic five-year plan.** Begin dreaming. If finances were unlimited, what would the nonprofit wish to accomplish over the next five years? How would a feature article in a national publication describe the organization's accomplishments five years from now?

- **Determine what it would take to make those dreams a reality.** After brainstorming to determine where the organization needs to be in five years, produce a brief outline of what will need to happen to make those dreams real—new facilities, new and improved equipment, or perhaps nationally recognized employees?

- **Begin sharing those dreams with individuals of wealth.** Identify those in the community or region who possess the ability to finance the organizational vision, and steadfastly involve them in shaping that vision. Seek their advice. Allow them to buy into the plans for significant achievement. Persistence will, in time, inspire these would-be donors and convince at least some of them to invest in the vision.

Many who have created wealth are big thinkers. They admire others who also think big. Sharing plans that will heighten the organization and its services will grab the attention of major gift prospects. Passion to reach for unheard of accomplishments will be contagious, and major gift prospects will invest with equal enthusiasm.

9

Campaign Themes do Matter

In planning and executing a campaign, it is important to give a great deal of thought to the slogan used throughout the duration of the campaign.

One way to establish a theme is to ask the following questions: Will the use of the funds be singular or multi-purpose? Who is the audience? Is the campaign running separate from other fund-raising efforts or will it include annual fund gifts, and perhaps, planned gift provisions? Are major gifts coming only from a smaller constituency or are all interested donors being approached, regardless of gift size? Are the funds for bricks and mortar or for programs?

How does timing fit into the campaign? Is the organization celebrating an anniversary? Will the campaign be tied to a previous fund-raising effort?

The answers to these and other questions will help to provide the basis for a slogan that will be 1) appropriate 2) impressionable, and 3) lasting.

Here are some slogans—both new and used—to consider when formulating one that best fits an organization's needs:

- Bridge to Distinction

- Foundation for the Second Century

- Building a Legacy of Love

- To Benefit Those Who Follow

- Hope for Tomorrow
- That Others Might Grow
- Leading the Way
- Decade for Growth
- Shared Vision for the Future
- Now More Than Ever
- Because We Care
- Bringing Strength to Our Future
- Pathway to Achievement
- Nurturing a New Generation
- Sustaining Our Commitment
- To Serve Those in Need
- To Build an Impregnable Future
- Building a Better Tomorrow
- Illuminating Our Future
- Design for the Next Decade

In advising a friend on "what to name the baby," a veteran mom suggested that the mom-to-be reexamine her nominations. The roster included the high and mighty, as well as the trendy and trite. Without criticism and with genuine concern the older mom counseled, "Why don't you go to the back porch and yell those names out loud and long." Returning from her assignment, the young friend looked across the table with new insight and remarked, "I see." Choosing a theme is no less momentous. Even after the campaign is complete, it will forever be referred to by its "given name." Choose one that conveys the distinctiveness of the organization, but also one that can be repeated with comfort and confidence—loud and long.

10

Project Analysis Rating Scale

An organization may need its electrical system rewired, but it would no doubt be unwise to fund the project with a campaign. Why? Because it has little or no appeal to prospective donors.

On the other hand, raising significant gifts for a new swimming pool complex because of its popularity, might be possible, but is that the nonprofit's most pressing need?

A Project Analysis Rating Scale provides one way of measuring and prioritizing which potential campaign projects are most needed and most apt to receive funding from a constituency.

Here is how it works: First, identify those needs perceived to be most critical by employees and assign a cost to each project. It would be wise to include some board members and major gift prospects in the process of identifying greatest needs. That way, they will begin to own, and perhaps fund, one or more of those needs at the appropriate time.

After identifying critical needs (as perceived internally), rank each project separately on the Project Analysis Rating Scale. Criteria used to rate and prioritize each project include:

- **Internal importance.** How does this project rank in importance with respect to all the organization's needs?

- **Donor attractiveness.** How attractive would this project be to potential donors? Is it, for instance, the type of project that would evoke strong emotion (like replacing a torn-down church steeple)?

- **Number of prospects.** Would the project have appeal to a large or small number of prospects?

- **Prospect financial ability.** Judge the financial ability of the prospect pool based on this project compared to the ability of a different group of prospects interested in another project. For instance, let us assume a college is measuring the fundability of a new social work lab as opposed to a new biology lab. The proposed biology lab prospect pool (which would include alumni who are medical professionals) would probably have greater financial ability than the social work alumni constituency.

- **Impact of completed project.** How many lives will the completed project affect?

- **Visibility of completed project.** Will the completion of the project be noticed by those served? Will it help the nonprofit to better market its services?

Criteria should be assigned a number based on perception. Each number is then multiplied by a weight factor. The results are added to give an overall ranking of the project's fundability and need as compared to other possible campaign projects.

The highest score a project could receive, based on this model, is 60 and the lowest possible score would be 12. Those projects with a 60-rating would be the most likely for a campaign.

Project Analysis Rating Scale

1. Rate each possible campaign project by assigning 1-5 in each category.

2. Multiply by the "weight" factor.

3. Add totals.

RATING SCALE
1 Very Low
2 Low
3 Average
4 Somewhat High
5 Very High

PROJECT BEING CONSIDERED FOR CAMPAIGN

DATE

Criteria	Score (1-5) X Weight = Total
Internal Importance	3
Donor Attractiveness	3
Number of Prospects	2
Prospects' Financial Ability	2
Impact of Completed Project	1
Visibility of Completed Project	1
GRAND TOTAL	

Highest Score = 60   Lowest Score = 12

11

The Case Statement Illustrates Why

A nonprofit's strategic plan serves as the "parent" to the case statement. The case statement documents the organization's vision and makes a compelling case for its funding. All subsequent campaign materials are an outgrowth of the case statement.

Because its purpose is often misunderstood, the following principles will help guide the development of a case statement:

- The process of writing a case statement, and involving prospects in drafting it, is at least as important as the finished product.

- The document should effectively communicate leadership's vision for the organization.

- It should reflect the institution's mission and be an outgrowth of the organization's strategic plan.

- A case statement forces agreement regarding an organization's priorities.

- It identifies genuine needs and offers practical solutions for meeting those needs.

- It should convey urgency.

- The completed case statement ensures that all constituents receive consistent messages about the organization's vision and priorities.

- The document identifies key themes and messages that will be useful in developing additional campaign materials, proposals and presentations.

- The case statement should be market driven—it should talk about satisfying donors' needs instead of the institution's needs.

- It should present a positive image of the organization.

- It should build on the organization's potential rather than past accomplishments.

- It should involve prospects.

- The document should demonstrate how gifts being sought will unleash the organization's potential and turn dreams into reality.

- It should be readable and credible.

- The case statement should provide a clear link between an organization's mission, its vision, and funding opportunities.

The finished case statement is part marketing and part strategic planning. It is an accurate blueprint of what is to come, seen through the eyes of those who strongly believe in and support the mission of the organization. Involve the most passionate supporters in the process and the result will be a case not only for advocacy, but also for affiliation.

12

The Case Statement Should Address Key Points

In developing and writing the organization's case statement, be sure to address the following key questions:

- **Why this organization?** The organization is competing with other nonprofits for gift support. There are a number of agencies offering similar kinds of services. What makes this organization more worthy of support?

- **Why these needs?** Even when donors are convinced that the organization is worthy of their support, what would compel them to address the needs that have been identified? Will the donor perceive his/her gift as making a difference?

- **Why now?** The case for support should demonstrate a sense of urgency.

- **Why me?** Finally, the case statement's message should require complete and sacrificial participation to fully realize the organization's vision.

Prospect Cultivation

Cultivation involves a series of well planned "moves" that lead the prospect from *awareness* to *interest* to *involvement* and, finally, to *commitment*.

Components of a Campaign

13

Endowment as a Part of Your Campaign

Endowment funds are the easiest funds to raise. Nonprofit organizations across the country are learning that the prescription for long-term success and stability is the creation of an endowment.

Many organizations review their annual fund support from year-to-year wondering how they will make another annual budget. The leadership likely remembers how difficult it was to raise sufficient funds for the construction of a facility or the renovation of current facilities. How can they expect those same donors to support an endowment?

The answer: endowment gifts generally are made using assets, not income. While the same is true of many capital funds efforts, the nature of a capital building campaign requires that a certain consistent level of cash flow must proceed at a designated rate. Therefore, while the desire for endowment may be very high, it does not have the same level of immediacy and demand as do both the annual and capital funds.

Common misunderstandings regarding endowments include:

- Endowment and estate gifts are the same thing.

- People do not want to give to endowments because the gifts cannot be "seen" like a building.

- Endowment prospects are hard to identify.

A rule of thumb is to review all of the institution's current donors and prospective donors. Those who can give a substantial gift through the use of income probably are good prospects for endowment gifts, but by no means do they comprise a comprehensive list of donors. Since endowment gifts generally occur from assets, other individuals who may have higher levels of assets and lower levels of annual income also are prospects. In addition, even small-gift donors may very well be good endowment donors because of their asset base over a long period of time.

It is important to provide the endowment donor a sense of permanence, perpetuity, and immortality.

- An annual gift evaporates over one year.

- A capital gift evaporates over the life of a particular building or piece of equipment.

- An endowment gift lasts forever in perpetuity.

The impact of an endowment gift can be experienced today, as well as to the day it is 100 years old. It would take a very uniquely structured building to provide the same level of service from the day it is dedicated to the day it is 100 years old.

In recent years, much confusion has occurred, because deferred gifts made through estates have commonly been called endowment gifts. While much endowment created in this country occurs as a result of a realized bequest, certainly that bequest could be specified for capital efforts or to supplement the annual operations of the institutions. Therefore, endowment is not strictly supplied through estate gifts.

A Definition

A simple definition of endowment is funds that are set aside with a portion of the earnings used to fund a particular activity of the institution. It is important from a stewardship perspective and is a fiduciary responsibility to make every good-faith effort to sustain the value of that endowment in perpetuity.

Endowment could be distinguished as a means to provide a permanent source of funding. As examples: John Harvard, who gave an endowment to create Harvard University; or Johns Hopkins, whose endowment created Johns Hopkins University and Hospital.

One institution received $1,000 in endowments in the late 1800s. All through the life of that institution they have been distributing all the earnings of those $1,000 endowments. Today, the endowments are as they were in 1878—

$1,000! It is not uncommon for 70 percent of the earnings to be distributed and 30 percent of the earnings put back into the fund to allow for growth. Therefore, a $100,000 gift or endowment made in 1994 will be worth an equivalent amount in the year 2004, 2044 and 2094.

The Impact

An endowment frequently causes misunderstanding among staff, volunteers, and friends of an institution. Even when the gift is made through an outright means—cash, stock, closely held securities, etc.—it may occur over a period of time. For example, a donor might make a $1 million endowment gift over a five-year period. Therefore, the endowment would grow to $200,000 the first year, $400,000 the second year, $600,000 the third year, $800,000 the fourth year, and $1 million at the end of the fifth year. The earnings would be about five or six percent of the amount endowed at the time. In this example, the recipient of those endowed funds would not see a full earning capacity for six years.

Earnings would occur over the six years and should either be incorporated or possibly distributed in increments during the earlier stages. Then the institution indicates it will distribute five percent as earnings or $50,000. The recipients see they have received $1 million, and yet have only $50,000 available to spend on equipment, staff, personnel, scholarships, etc.

The importance of endowment is not that they have $50,000 to spend in that one year; it is that they will have $50,000 or its equivalent to spend each year forever. Over the next 10 years, that gift will be $500,000. Over the next 50 years, the gift will be the equivalent of $2.5 million. Over the next 100 years, it will be the equivalent of $5 million.

The Donors

Let us review what kind of donor makes a gift to endowments. There are numerous examples. Here are several. (Fictitious names have been used to protect confidentiality.)

John and Winnie Borden

John and Winnie made a gift to their alma mater to endow a school of education. The gift was $10 million. John had not been able to receive an education. In fact, he would joke that his success had come through "learning at the knee of others." He knew the importance of education. What better way to perpetuate that value than to fund a school of education?

John and Winnie had a difficult life. They lost two children to accidental death. They understood the impact of mortality and the demand for immortality. They understood what permanence and perpetuity really meant.

They used current assets, an income-generating asset and an estate vehicle to fund their $10 million endowment gift. First, they made an outright gift of $3 million to be paid over a three-year period. Secondly, they placed $2 million in a charitable lead trust, which ran for a period of 10 years. The earnings from the charitable lead trust were eight percent per year, $160,000 annually or $1.6 million for the 10-year period. Finally, John funded the remaining $5.4 million through his estate to come to the university at the time of his death ($2.7 million) and at the time of Winnie's death ($2.7 million).

Did the Bordens give a $10 million endowment for a school of education? They certainly believe they did. They structured their gift in such a manner as to allow the school of education a guaranteed cash flow forever, beginning slowly and increasing as time passes.

Milicent North

Milicent gave a small, annual donation to a child-care agency—only a few hundred dollars each year. After her husband's passing, she discovered the importance of this child-care agency to her life.

The agency was conducting a building campaign and she made a gift of $50,000. Upon reflection, she thought it would be important to have an endowment in support of that facility, so she changed her will to reflect a $200,000 bequest to endow the facility.

Milicent, at 85, had never taken a full inventory of her financial wealth. She discovered she was worth a great deal more than she ever believed. Her philanthropy is far from over.

Harlan George

Harlan and his wife lived near an organization for disabled adults and children. He had lived there for more than 40 years. Harlan had never made a gift to the agency. He had never even been on the grounds.

One evening, in an effort to extend appreciation to its neighbors, the agency invited them to a reception. For the first time, Harlan visited the campus. One of the members of the development committee recognized Harlan. Harlan was not a man of great wealth, but had been a good steward of his resources. He had invested well and lived modestly.

Following that first meeting, the agency leadership spent a great deal of time expressing to Harlan his importance to the institution. They asked for advice and used most of it. They discussed the future as well as the past.

Ultimately, Harlan gave the child-care agency $597,000, which included a life estate on his home and a life-insurance policy of $25,000. The remainder was held in trust at a local bank. Harlan gave the gift because the organization was a good neighbor accomplishing good things.

The use of cash, the beginning of an endowment and the small corpus built over a number of years, are traditional means to creating an endowment. But it is important to encourage donors to review their assets including collectibles, hobbies, land holdings, rental properties, stocks—and finally, their estates.

The key is to find a way for a gift today to become a significant gift tomorrow. Accomplish that, and everyone wins.

14

Essential Tips on Securing Governmental Grants

An organization has a great idea for a program that will change the lives of many people in a positive way. The research is completed. The need for services is documented. Clients are identified and ready to participate in the program.

What is the missing ingredient? Funding. It has not been secured nor identified. Now what? The following tips will help identify the funding sources open to a program idea. It will also give critical information to help secure those funds through a competitive application process. Follow these tips and programs will be up and running soon!

Identifying Potential Funding Sources

The easiest way to learn about grant competitions from state and federal agencies is to ask individual departments (i.e., state Department of Public Health, federal Department of Education) to include the organization on their mailing lists. Departments will send announcements of available funds and often send the entire Request for Proposal (RFP) to everyone on the mailing list.

Another way to receive information is to belong to an organized group that represents the agency's target population or program area. For example, the National Network for Runaway Youth has regional organizations and one of its goals is to keep its member agencies updated on new funding opportunities.

A federal publication, *The Federal Register,* is another source of information. Published Monday through Friday, (excluding federal holidays) this publication includes the daily actions of Congress and grant announcements for federal funds. Subscribe to *The Federal Register* or find it at most public libraries.

Before Writing

After locating a funding opportunity through a governmental source, there are some key questions to answer before starting the proposal. Read the RFP carefully to answer these questions:

1) **Is the agency or program eligible to submit a proposal?** If the agency will only support state organizations and this is a private agency, it will not be eligible. Do not apply.

2) **Do the potential funder's goals match the goals of the project?** Is it a stretch? Is it necessary to change the program's goals to match those of the funding source?

   For example, if a program's goal is to prepare high school students for continued education in a four-year institution and the funding agency's program goal is to prepare high school students for work upon graduation, is it possible to change from a college-preparatory program to a vocational-education program? If the answer is no, then do not apply for the funding.

   In some instances, it may be feasible to change the program's goals. However, the danger in changing the program to meet potential grant opportunities is that it may no longer address the needs already identified.

3) **Can the agency carry out the grant under the funder's guidelines?** Can the agency meet the funder's requirements, both financially and programmatically? If the funder requires a staff-client ratio of 1-to-5, and the agency has a 1-to-10 ratio, can the funder's standards be met? If not, do not submit the application.

4) **Can the matching requirements be met under the budget?** Is the funding available to meet cash-match requirements? Can the agency's accounting system track in-kind support? Do not make promises in the application that the agency is not equipped to deliver.

Answering yes to these questions probably means the agency is ready to proceed with preparing an application.

Reading the Request for Proposal (RFP)

Although RFPs are unique to each governmental agency, there are similarities in what funders are asking for in proposals. Here is a list of what can be expected in most RFPs:

- **Abstract.** A brief description of the program, target group, goals and objectives, time frame, and amount of money requested.

- **Statement of need.** It should answer these questions: What is the need? Why is there a need? How great is the need? Give statistics, if available. For example, specify the number of children living in poverty, the increase in teenage pregnancies, or the number of families victimized by disasters. Make a strong case for the project.

- **Program description.** An overview of how the agency will address the need or solve the problems described in the need section. Some funders may require that this section be divided to include methodology, time lines, and/or procedures. The instructions for completing the RFP should state exactly what kind of information to be included. However, never guess what the funder wants. When in doubt call the number given for technical assistance, clarification, or further information.

- **Goals and objectives.** List the goals and objectives for the project. Goals are the ultimate changes the organization would like to see occur, often written more abstractly. For instance the goal could read, "Increase the number of young women enrolled in a four-year degree program." Objectives must be measurable and within a given time frame, and written in a way that is outcome oriented. The objectives are the steps needed to accomplish and achieve the goals. For example, an objective to the goal stated above could be, "Fifty young women will graduate with a high school diploma in May 1999."

- **Background.** Describe the agency's qualifications in carrying out the proposed project. What knowledge, skills or experience does the agency and staff bring to the project and to the proposed target audience? Many funders request additional information such as a copy of an organizational chart of the agency, a list of the board of directors, a copy of the most recent audit or financial statement, and proof of 501(c)(3) status.

53

- **Dissemination.** How will the information gained through the project be transferred to others in the field? For example, will it be published and distributed in a how-to manual? Will the agency participate in a national conference or establish a network to provide others with technical assistance?

- **Evaluation.** This could be requested in two ways. One is an overview of how the overall effectiveness of the program will be evaluated. Another is how each specific objective will be evaluated. If there are measurable objectives, the evaluation section should be relatively easy to prepare. Outside evaluators may be proposed. If so, be sure to include the cost in the budget.

- **Budget.** This must include a total budget for the project, listed by line item, which shows the amount requested from the funder. Most budget sections should include a complete breakdown of each line item. For example:

  Telephone $50/month x 12 months = $600
  Coordinator $25,000/year x 50% of time = $12,500

- **Signature Forms.** An agency representative (the CEO or Board Chair) must sign the cover page and various assurances. Be sure these are complete. Check the RFP carefully. Federal agencies may even specify the color of ink to be used for signatures.

Other components. Funders sometimes request additional information, such as:

1) **Time line.** Usually in a chart format, highlighting when key events of the project will take place.

2) **Approach.** A more detailed description of how the project will be conducted. This section usually expands upon the narrative.

3) **Staffing pattern and experience.** A description of how the project will be staffed and the qualifications of those staff members already employed.

4) **Letters of support or commitment.** These should be from individuals outside the organization who know the program and services. Letters of commitment should describe how the individuals intend to work with the project.

5) **Table of Contents.** This is not always required but is an added tool to help the reviewer. The table of contents should highlight the sections listed above.

Writing Style

Before writing, study the criteria that will be used by the reviewer. The criteria, also found in the RFP, provide additional information in helping prepare the proposal. This is the information the grant reviewer will be looking for when reading the proposal. While preparing the application remember to:

- **Write the proposal assuming the reviewer knows nothing about the agency or program** (because they probably do not). Avoid acronyms.

- **Write a realistic program.** If the project sounds too good to be possible, the reviewer will sense this and the score will suffer. Also, if the proposal shoots for the moon and then receives funding, the organization will have to deliver on its promises.

- **Be reader friendly.** Do not add fluff (also known as bull). Be clear and concise.

Address each section of the RFP thoroughly. Answer any and all questions posed.

Visual Appearance

The key to a successful application is keeping the reviewer reading the proposal. Make it easy for him or her to read. Whenever, possible, use plenty of white space, large type, and headings. Always remember a reviewer has more than one application to review. If a proposal is number eight in a pile of 20, and it is difficult to read, chances are the reviewer will read the summary section only and skim the rest of the document. Keep the following points in mind when preparing a proposal.

- **Organize the proposal in sections as presented in the RFP.** If the application outlines sections as Need, Program, Goals and Objectives, Evaluation, use those same words in the headings. Then highlight each section title, either by underlining, bolding, or enlarging the print.

- **Make sure the proposal is typed, proofed, and easy to read.** Remember that the proposal is competing with stacks of applications. If the proposal is difficult to read (either visually or conceptually) the reviewer may not finish the entire document. Obviously, the score will suffer.

- **Number the pages.**

- **Ask someone not connected or involved with the project to critically review the proposal before it is submitted.** This will help assure that the proposal is clear.

Summary

When these steps are followed, the chance for submitting a winning proposal will be remarkably increased. Grant writing does not need to be complicated. Research the potential funder and make sure the match between what is to be funded and what the grantor wants to fund is a good one.

Then, follow the guidelines. Is this a simple process? Not always, but by using the directions in the Request for Proposal as a road map, it will be easier. By the time the proposal is completed and sent to the funder, the Request for Proposal should be worn out. Sections should be highlighted, circled in red ink, and the pages crinkled! It is the most essential tool available to explain what the funder wants to fund.

Funds obtained through state or federal programs can help strengthen, expand or develop new ways of helping others. There are many opportunities to apply for grants. Use these tips to identify and secure the ones that fit the organization's specific programs.

15

The ABCs of Grant Writing

The following represents an Always Be Certain checklist consisting of a dozen suggestions:

1. **Know the reason behind the grant application.** As obvious as this may seem, it is the number one step in writing a competitive grant. If an institution does not have a clear plan that provides the reason for writing the grant, applying will simply be "chasing the money" rather than advancing the mission of the institution. Or, as a volunteer once said, "You cannot sell from an empty shell." If the grant does not have substance and purpose, and if it does not complement the bigger picture the organization has for its future, it will be difficult to write a successful grant. This is the time to write a case for support. If the case does not make sense, the proposal will probably not make sense to the foundation. Explain in clear, easily understood language how the grant will significantly advance the mission of the organization. If this message is not clear, do not write it.

2. **Do the homework.** At a Council for the Advancement and Support of Education (CASE) conference on foundations and grant writing, the guest speakers were representatives from foundations. Some of the speakers were foundation presidents; others were program

officers. The speakers did not mince words regarding a need to do the homework before approaching a foundation. They made it abundantly clear that if an organization does not care enough to find out about the foundation's interests, then its grant proposal will probably end up in "file 13." What they referred to as a "shotgun" approach to grant writing was the worst offense of all. The lesson here is to carefully research the foundation, paying attention to its criteria for support before proceeding.

3. **Read the entire grant application.** Someone has taken the time to write the grant application. He or she has been selective in choosing the information to receive and the sequence in which to receive it. Take time to read every sentence of the application; then write the grant request in response to the information asked. Do exactly as requested. For example, do the trustees want the grant request to be typed doubled-spaced? Are the number of pages limited? What about requested support materials (most recent audit, 501(c)3 letter, and list of Board of Directors)? How many copies are required?

   If a foundation does not have a grant application, make a phone call to confirm the information to be included in a grant request. If a foundation indicates a preference for a letter proposal before deciding whether or not to have a full proposal submitted, follow instructions explicitly.

4. **Check the spelling.** While this may seem to be a technical, computer activity, remember that spell-check does not catch words spelled correctly but used inappropriately in the proposal. For example, in a grant proposal in support of a special event where a guest chef was invited, along with his assistant (in cooking circles, known as the sous chef), the secretary had written, "accompanied by his soused chef." Which, of course, is not the same. Along these lines, always present a neatly-typed proposal, on clean paper, in a font size that a person with normal eyesight can read.

5. **Send the proposal to a specific person.** Regardless of the research necessary, get the name and title of the person to whom the proposal should be addressed. Never use "Dear Sir or Madam" or "To Whom It May Concern."

6. **Adhere to the deadline.** The old saying about a "day late and a dollar short" is absolutely true when missing a foundation's deadline. If there are doubts about the date, call the foundation. If a

grant requires a response confirming an acceptance of the terms, respond immediately. One organization received a challenge grant for several hundred thousand dollars from The J.E. and L.E. Mabee Foundation in Tulsa, Oklahoma. This is a great foundation. Their guidelines are well written, as are their instructions for the signed, returned agreement indicating acceptance of the conditions of their challenge grant within a certain number of days. The organization's director of development, perhaps caught up in the excitement of receiving such a wonderful grant, failed to have the form signed and did not get it returned in the allotted time. They lost the challenge grant. That is probably enough said on this subject.

7. **Keep the proposal people-centered.** A building is not what is interesting to a foundation. It may be necessary to achieve within a campaign, but ultimately it is only a place where people can be better served by the organization. When writing a grant to support a program or service, write about the people who will benefit because this program or service exists.

8. **Have measurable outcomes.** It is not enough to say, "more people are being served than ever before." Instead, foundations are interested in what happened to the increased number of people served. Have their lives improved? How has this been evaluated? Were they asked if the services were what they needed? Was information tracked after a period of time to confirm that services or programs sustained their improvement?

9. **Demonstrate the sustainability of the project.** If a new facility is involved, how will the organization pay for maintenance and upkeep? If a new program or service is being created, how will it be maintained after the grant expires?

10. **Secure external validation for the grant request.** Foundations are more interested in what others outside of the organization think than self-assessments. Letters of support written specifically in support of a grant request validate that others know and value the organization. These letters should also be addressed to the appropriate person at the foundation—not to the nonprofit. (This does not mean that supporters mail the letters directly to the foundation. The letters should be included with the grant request.)

11. **Indicate the intent to collaborate with others.** Organizations that do not indicate the intent to collaborate with other organizations

to strengthen the outcome of the project drastically reduce their chances for writing a competitive grant. Referring to the organization's efforts as unique sends up a red flag that often signals a lack of awareness of what other organizations are doing elsewhere. With the availability of this type of information on the World Wide Web, organizations must be very careful. Remember the numerous requests that foundations receive. Foundation trustees have read about similar organizations and they know that the probability of proposing something unique is rare.

12. **Thank the foundation for its support.** It is hard to believe, but true. Some organizations fail to thank foundations after receiving a grant. Imagine how that makes the foundation officers feel. And thanking them once is not enough. Keeping them informed about the progress of the project, and the support received from others, helps them know that their investment in the organization was a wise one. The golden rule in fund raising that prior donors are always the best prospects also holds true in the relationship with foundations.

Foundations exist to help change society for the better. And while it is true they are required by law to appropriate a percentage of their earnings to qualified organizations, they are not ATM machines. Treat them with respect and always be good stewards of the funds they have entrusted to the organization.

16

Making Annual Fund a Part of the Campaign

The goal for The Cerebral Palsy Research Foundation (CPRF) of Wichita, Kansas was to raise $250,000 in unrestricted annual giving. If CPRF could garner and maintain that level of support, essentially they would develop the equivalent of a $5 million endowment. (A common income distribution level from endowment is 5 percent.)

Historically, CPRF has enjoyed sporadic fund-raising success. Annual fund raising has ranged from $30,000 to $60,000 occasionally moving to $100,000 due to an estate gift.

To secure the annual fund, the following areas were reviewed:

1. **Volunteers.** What were the opportunities for volunteers and who had already been engaged?

2. **Consistency.** The messages provided by CPRF had varied over the years and the organization needed a consistent message to give to its donor base.

3. **Preparation for future board membership.** There were a small number of individuals who could succeed a board that, while still relatively young, would soon need successors.

4. **Prospect research.** CPRF knew little about many of its previous donors.

5. **CEO support.** There was extraordinary CEO support for a strong annual fund.

6. **Board support.** The board of directors was anxious to build a broader base.

7. **Impact of organization.** CPRF had become an important resource, but was not as well recognized as it deserved.

8. **Recognition and acknowledgement of donors.** While there had been recognition and acknowledgement, there was not a systematic strategy.

9. **Staff involvement.** Program staff involvement in fund raising had been limited.

Analysis of the last five years of giving indicated that, while there had been a spiking of gifts throughout that five-year period, essentially annual fund support amounted to an average of $50,000. The recommendation was to develop a two-tiered approach to reach a $250,000 level.

"In the first year, we raised $125,000 in annual fund support, an increase of $75,000. In the second year, we were able to raise $250,000," said Dan Carney, Chairman of the Board for CPRF.

The following elements were created with input from members of the CPRF program staff to determine their needs and to develop a greater understanding of how gifts would be used:

1. A review of the existing budget was conducted to determine the elements being funded through unrestricted giving. These could be separated and characterized to donors as restricted gifts because of a specific impact.

2. The creation of an Annual Fund Advisory Panel, utilizing successful men and women from the business community of Wichita.

3. A broadening of the prospect base through the relationships and contacts of the members of the Annual Fund Advisory Committee.

4. Preparation for each solicitation by ensuring volunteers they have strong support for each solicitation and that they are not just thrown into the community asking for gifts.

5. Regular reports to the Board and Annual Fund Advisory Committee on the success of the annual fund.

6. Provision of an opportunity for recognition and acknowledgement throughout this process. CPRF recognized donors through the Unity of Purpose dinner. This annual event was broadened to recognize the success of the organization.

7. Construction of a prospect database to better understand donors and their motivations for giving.

8. A request in the second year for multi-year pledges to allow donor appeal.

9. Creation of matching gifts and challenge gift opportunities so donors know their dollars will be used in a broader appeal.

The above activities and objectives have allowed CPRF to grow from an annual fund of $50,000 to more than $300,000 in only two years. "We found that members of the community were unaware of the role of CPRF," said Mike Burrus, president of Multimedia Cablevision and chair of the Annual Fund Advisory Board. "Once we were able to explain the role, we found that individuals in Wichita were ready to step forward, which has resulted in our success."

17

Public/Private Partnerships

$\mathbf{T}$oday, it is increasingly important for nonprofits to pursue new funding vehicles to assist an organization in reaching its mission. One of the most innovative ways to secure large gifts for capital costs and endowment revenues is through partnerships with governmental agencies, such as a municipal or county government.

Across the country, partnerships between nonprofits and governmental agencies are being used to fund a wide range of important projects, including performing arts centers, youth sports complexes, indoor aquatic centers, railroad and history museums, zoos, and other needed facilities. In many instances, gifts of property taxes, sales tax revenues, or other public revenue sources in excess of $1 million and more are being received.

Benefits to Nonprofits

Partnerships with governmental organizations can provide numerous benefits to nonprofit agencies. The most important benefits include:

- Access to new and large sources of cash gifts for capital projects

- Access to borrowing money at very low interest rates

- Opportunities to lease undeveloped public land to build new facilities

- Seed money for funding campaign assessments
- Long-term sources of revenue for operational maintenance
- Assistance with infrastructure improvements, such as improved streets, water, and lighting systems

Benefits to Public Agencies

Similarly, partnerships with nonprofit organizations can provide numerous benefits to municipal governments, school systems, state and federal agencies, and other public providers. The most important benefits include:

1. Opportunities to broaden citizen involvement and volunteering

2. Increased access to philanthropic gifts for leveraging with tax revenues

   a. Access to a broader base of nonprofit management expertise for operating programs

   b. Opportunities for reducing long-term tax costs to operate programs and services

   c. The ability to outsource responsibilities for directly providing services that may be of a lower priority than core governmental activities, i.e., police, fire, street maintenance, etc.

Case Study: The Topeka Performing Arts Center

In Topeka, Kansas, the community used a creative partnership between the Topeka Performing Arts Association and the City to plan, fund, and manage the development of a state-of-the-art performing arts center.

Topeka is a community of 125,000 residents. While a number of nonprofits were involved with theater, symphony, dance, and other performing arts activities, the City had no suitable facility to present these activities.

In 1986, a small group of private citizens approached the mayor of the city with an idea to study the feasibility of converting the city's existing municipal auditorium (built in 1939) into a performing arts center. Based on this idea, the City allocated a sum of $30,000 which was used to fund a campaign assessment regarding development of such a facility, including the potential use of a public/private partnership to finance and operate the Center. A project manager, working with a citizen task force of 22 members, was appointed.

Over the next 12 months, the task force worked with other dedicated community members and city staff, studying the feasibility for developing such a performing arts center. Issues such as potential customer markets, the redesign of the facility, the structure of a management board, operating costs, capital costs for redesign, and recommended sources of public and private revenues to fund the project were analyzed.

Recommendations from the study centered on the City's renovation of the existing municipal auditorium into a 2,300-seat performing arts center, with additional space for rehearsals, classrooms, and community events. For the estimated $5 million in costs for the Center, $2.5 million was to come from tax dollars and be matched by proceeds of a $2.5 million fund-raising campaign. The performing arts center would be managed by a not-for-profit board, which would enter into a long-term lease with the City for operations of the Center.

The task force's recommendations were approved by the City, and an architect was hired to proceed with the performing arts center's design. A consulting firm was retained to work with the Performing Arts Center's Board of Trustees on the $2.5 million campaign. Approximately 18 months later, the leadership reached the campaign goal, plus an additional $400,000. In March of 1991, the Topeka Performing Arts Center opened and has since been in continuous operation.

15 Questions to Answer Before Securing Major Public Gifts

The cultivation, solicitation, and management of major gifts from public agencies is just as important as the process for securing gifts from private individuals, foundations or businesses. Just as these organizations and individuals want to know the purposes for and uses of their gifts, so will a public agency. Be prepared to answer any or all of the following 15 questions when requesting a gift of tax revenues for a campaign.

1. **"For what community purposes will the revenues be used?"** Elected officials want to ensure that tax revenues will be directed to programs and services that serve public purposes. Be prepared to illustrate the benefits of the project to both the entire community and to specific segments of the community if applicable.

2. **"What will the total campaign goal be, and how was the goal determined?"** As with other larger donors, public officials will want to know the total amount of funds to be raised through the campaign, as well as the nature of those funds, i.e., for capital projects, endowments, etc. Similar to other donors, public officials are often interested in the basis for the fund-raising projections and the analysis process that was followed.

67

3. **"How much of a gift will be required and over how long a time?"** Just like other donors, public officials are interested in knowing the specific nature of the request and how long of a period they have to make the gift.

4. **"Can these efforts save tax dollars, and if so how?"** More and more elected officials are looking at investing tax dollars for sound business reasons as well as public purposes. If an organization can show that the gift can reduce taxes over the long run, such as building a needed youth sports complex that can be run by a volunteer board and coaches, it will have a greater chance of receiving the gift.

5. **"How much of the total costs for the campaign will be supported through the public gift?"** Public officials are generally more interested in leveraging tax revenues as a smaller part of a project and with other sources of revenue than they are in contributing tax revenues as the sole source, or the principal source, for funding a project.

6. **"Who is the agency's primary customer base?"** Governmental agencies are generally more supportive of gifts to projects that serve customers living in their communities or political boundaries. Be prepared with records of where customers live and work when making a solicitation for a public gift.

7. **"How supportive is the community of the organization receiving a gift of tax revenues?"** Public officials like to make gifts that are popular in their political jurisdictions. Be prepared to show community support for making the gift. Nonprofits can use statistically valid phone and mail surveys as sources of public information to measure public support of their efforts.

8. **"What are other actual and potential sources of gifts, and in what amounts?"** Public officials often like to know what other foundations, individuals, and businesses in the community or their political area are supportive of the campaign. Be prepared to furnish this information within the confidentiality guidelines established by the campaign and donors.

9. **Who will be the leaders of this fund-raising campaign?** Public officials particularly are interested in projects that are backed by well-known and respected residents.

10. **"In what other services or programs does the agency partici-pate?"** Particularly if the campaign is to fund a new service, pub-lic officials may be interested in other activities and programs with which the nonprofit is involved.

11. **"What is the game plan if the campaign goal is not reached?"** While the objective of all campaigns is to reach the goal, some-times this does not occur. Public officials need to know up front what the contingency plans will be, and how it will affect their gift.

12. **"Is this a one-time gift or will there be future requests?"** Public officials will want to know if the organization plans to come back to them for future gifts, or if this will be a one-time solicitation. Like private donors, public officials often are willing to fund some ongoing expenses relating to their gifts for campaigns.

13. **"Will financial records be open to public auditors?"** This question is of particular importance, not only from a public policy stand-point, but also as an issue of legality.

14. **"Will services be open to all residents of the community or lim-ited in some ways?"** Public dollars flow more readily to cam-paigns that provide services open to all community residents. In fact, this objective may be used as an appeal to have part of the public gift fund a scholarship program or other vehicles allowing for full public access.

15. **"Is the board open to accepting public officials as members?"** On some occasions, the public body making the gift may ask for some type of representation on the board, either as a member or more frequently in a quasi-official manner. While these requests are infrequent, be prepared with an answer.

Concluding Comments

For an increasing number of nonprofits, major gifts through public sec-tor partnerships have become a viable source for raising revenues for campaigns and funding ongoing operating costs.

Similar to other major donors, public agencies want to invest their money wisely, and they want to positively impact their residents and commu-nity. Many nonprofits have much to offer public agencies and they should cer-tainly consider a public sector partnership as an opportunity to broaden and increase their fund-raising base.

18

Seek Out Opportunities to Establish Challenge Gifts

Seeking "lead gifts"—the "quiet" or unannounced phase of a campaign—will determine the size, scope, and ultimate success of the effort. The gifts solicited during this phase should account for 40 to 70 percent of the overall campaign goal.

One or more donors issue challenge gifts to leverage their giving—since additional contributions are matched. If an institution can raise a specified amount from other donors over an agreed-to period of time, the challenge is met and gifts are essentially doubled.

It pays to seek out challenge gift opportunities. Consider the following:

- **Individuals.** Whether approaching a new prospect or an existing donor for a challenge gift, know that this feature can be used to help leverage a major gift. The person's intended gift will receive a great deal of publicity and will help to encourage others to contribute.

- **Groups of individuals.** Sometimes it is difficult to raise the needed challenge from one source. If that is the case, consider a challenge made up of multiple donors.

- **Board of Directors.** There are times when a board challenge can provide the impetus for others' giving. In fact, there are times when a challenge from one board member can motivate the remaining board members to contribute sacrificially.

- **Businesses and corporations.** Businesses often appreciate the visibility resulting from a major gift. A challenge gift from a business would certainly bring added visibility and contribute to the image of the business as an upstanding corporate leader.

- **Foundations.** Some foundations actually base giving decisions on whether grants will be used as challenges to leverage gifts from others. These foundations are often motivated to participate in projects that might not otherwise be successfully completed without their assistance.

Capital Campaigns

Real life examples of capital campaign successes are presented in chapters 44-55 to illustrate the organization of a capital campaign and how they work with operating support, endowment, and the public sector. See these chapters for detailed capital campaign strategies.

Prioritizing & Managing Your Prospects

19

Prioritize Prospects

In spite of increasingly sophisticated methods of rating and screening major gift prospects, there are tried-and-tested ways that any non-profit can utilize.

Take the method devised by Karel Walls. While she was working as a prospect researcher at a biomedical research institution, she developed a Prospect Classification Matrix as a way of sorting the "suspects" from the "prospects."

Here is how it works. The person responsible for rating and screening prospects considers each prospect individually and rates him or her based on eight weighted criteria. Those characteristics considered more important in the rating process receive a higher weight factor.

The eight weighted factors include:

1. **Assets (15 points).** While assets alone do not determine the likelihood of receiving a major gift, they are certainly a necessary ingredient in the realization of one.

2. **Former donor (30 points).** Has the individual made a gift to the organization within the past three years?

3. **Relationship (15 points).** Does this person have a relationship with the organization—former board member, graduate, grateful patient, client?

4. **Access (20 points).** How accessible is the individual to the organization or someone connected to the organization? For example, is the prospect a friend of someone within the institution? Does the individual serve on a board with someone from the organization?

5. **Interest (10 points).** Has the prospect requested information from the organization? Is he or she currently on the mailing list?

6. **Proximity (5 points).** Does the individual reside or conduct business in the area, or is he or she known to contribute to other organizations in the area?

7. **Giving pattern (3 points).** Does the person contribute to organizations with a similar mission?

8. **Philanthropy (2 points).** Is the individual known to be generous to other causes?

Walls points out, "Although it was rare that anyone would get a perfect score of 100, those with a total score of 60 or more would be considered viable prospects."

Profiles were developed on those who received high scores and the names were listed in a descending numerical order and used as a basis for peer review and strategic planning sessions.

Prospect Classification Matrix

Name	Assets	Giving History	Relation-ship	Access	Interest	Prox-imity	Giving Pattern	Philan-thropic	Total
	15 Points	*30 Points*	*15 Points*	*20 Points*	*10 Points*	*5 Points*	*3 Points*	*2 Points*	*100 Points*
Phil Anthropic	15		15	20	10		3	2	65
I.M. Rich	15	30		20		5		2	72
U.R. Wealthy	15		15	20	10	5	3		68
Minnie Bags	15					5	3	2	25

Here is another example of a prospect rating form. This form serves as a way of measuring both an individual's ability and likelihood to make a major gift.

Criteria used to rate prospects on this form include:

1. **Common interests.** Does the prospect exhibit interest in the kinds of objectives the organization attempts to address?

2. **Financial ability.** Can the prospect afford a major gift?

3. **Commitment to philanthropy.** Does the prospect have a history of giving to other causes?

4. **Commitment to the organization.** Has the prospect exhibited any past commitment to the organization (i.e., past contributor or participant in previous programs or events)?

5. **Linkages with the organization.** Has the prospect held an office in the nonprofit or been served as a client of the organization? Does he or she have friends or family who have a relationship with the organization?

6. **Time window.** Is it the right time for the prospect to make a major gift? Examples affecting a time window might include inheritance, sale of certain assets, divorce, and age.

7. **Personality.** How can the individual's personality affect his or her interest in making a gift? Is the individual driven by a strong ego? Is he or she caring? Personality traits will influence the likelihood of giving.

8. **Past solicitation success.** Has the prospect contributed to the organization in the past? Is there a long or brief history of giving? Has she/he made a previous major gift?

9. **Politics and philosophy.** Do the political and philosophical beliefs of this individual coincide with the mission and goals of the organization? Does the prospect stand far to the left or right politically? Where is the nonprofit positioned politically?

Weights are assigned to each rating criterion and then added. In this case, the highest possible score one can receive is 85.

Prospect Rating Form

Prospect _____ **Date** _____

Directions: 1. Rate each prospect 1-5 in each category
("5" is the highest rating one can receive).
2. Multiply each criteria by the weight factor.
3. Add totals

Criteria	Score (1-5)	Weight	Total
Common Interests		2	
Financial Ability		3	
Commitment to Philanthropy		1	
Commitment to our Organization		3	
Linkages with our Organization		1	
Time Window		3	
Personality		1	
Past Solicitation Success		2	
Common Politics/Philosophy		1	
		Grand Total Highest Score = 85	

20

Evaluate Ways to Prioritize Prospects

Whether preparing for a campaign, selecting prospect groups for a phonathon, or simply evaluating an organization's fund-raising potential, prioritizing prospects can be a solution for making the most of staff time and efforts. Prioritizing prospects will keep a campaign focused on those who exhibit the greatest *potential* as well as the greatest *likelihood* of contributing.

There are many ways to group the donor and prospect base, and several techniques which generate similar results. The following summary can be used to navigate the major parts of this process and help reveal the "cream of the crop."

Goal Setting

With any major project, the first step is to define the goals:

- Is the organization preparing for a major or annual campaign, embarking on a direct mail solicitation program, or setting up a group to be contacted for a phone-a-thon? The end product will determine the target group and will define the search criteria.

- How large a group of donors is needed to fulfill the fund-raising goal? Keep in mind the number of staff and volunteers needed to manage those prospects.

79

- What sizes of gifts are expected from the donors in this group? Anticipating both the number and range of gift sizes will help determine the approach taken in selecting methods of prospect prioritization.

Internal Reports

One of the easiest and most effective methods for prioritizing prospects is through the use of computer reports designed in-house.

- Delineate the donor base by past giving levels, consistency, types, and programs.

- Group together those with similar professions, age ranges, geographic locations or interests.

- Designate groups with board memberships.

- Indicate volunteer relationships.

- Set aside the organization's faculty and/or staff for a separate campaign component.

Electronic Screening

Several vendors offer a variety of electronic screening services. If you feel the data you have in-house is insufficient, you have several options for obtaining additional information on your prospects and donors. Costs and data analysis services vary with each vendor.

Screening and Rating Sessions

Using the results from internal reports or electronic screening services, refine the list of prospects by conducting screening and rating sessions. These are meetings set up with various groups to rate the potential giving of prospects they know. To set up a session:

- Gather board members, key community leaders and donors, regional groups, and those with similar professions or backgrounds.

- Design simple, multiple-choice report formats which volunteers can easily fill out in a short period of time. The session should be focused and not last more than two or three hours.

- Solicit only enough information to identify the prospects.

- Keep the number of prospects to be rated to a manageable number. Match up the group to be rated with the group doing the rating. Volunteers should be familiar with the prospects in their reports.

Involve Researchers from the Start

The key to success in any of these procedures is to involve the research staff in the project from the very beginning.

- Get input from all development staff at the planning stage.

- Make sure researchers participate in the process and attend all rating sessions. They can document any additional details which might be discussed, and help interpret reports for the volunteers.

- Allow enough time and staff to follow up on the results of these projects. The ability to use the data once it is collected is as important as having the data.

- Determine up front who will be responsible for analyzing the data once it is collected. Some of the electronic screening vendors offer varying levels of analysis support as part of their services.

- Decide how the staff will use the data. Divide the prioritized prospect pool among staff members as soon as possible, and set goals and deadlines.

21

Measuring the Constituency's Gift Potential

Being able to estimate a constituency's gift potential at any given time plays a crucial role in planning the organization's future and projecting how that future will be funded.

In order to determine the institution's overall gift potential, however, rate and screen the constituency. The process of rating and screening individuals, businesses, and foundations allows an organization to categorize prospects based on estimates of the individuals' financial worth and giving potentials.

There are various rules of thumb for estimating giving ability. One guideline states, "If a prospect is well cultivated, highly motivated, and effectively solicited, she/he can be expected to contribute 5 percent of annual income over a five-year period or 10 percent of net worth over the same period."

An individual with a $60,000 income would, for example, be likely to contribute $3,000 (5 percent) over five years. An individual with a net worth of $500,000 would be capable of donating $50,000 (10 percent) over a five-year period.

Unlike the above rule of thumb, another guideline is not based on a specific percentage of income or net worth. Rather, it includes a number of additional factors, like past giving history, timing, the donor's ability to replace assets, etc., to be considered in addition to the donor's financial ability.

Once individuals' giving potentials have been determined and categorized, the next step is to determine how many prospects need to be identified in each financial category in order to achieve the desired funding goal.

A rule of thumb to measure the number of prospects that need to be cultivated and approached is that it will generally take at least three qualified prospects for each single gift secured at each giving level.

Based on that principle, compare the existing number of prospects in each giving category with the number of prospects required to achieve the desired campaign goal.

This comprehensive process of rating and screening prospects and then projecting the number of additional prospects needed, will help determine what remains to be accomplished in order to reach the desired funding goal.

Rule of Thumb #1:

If the prospect is well cultivated, highly motivated and effectively solicited, she or he could be expected to contribute 5 percent of annual income over a five-year period or 10 percent of the individual's net worth over the same five-year period.

The table below represents another method which can be used to measure an individual's gift potential. Unlike the above, it is not based on a consistent percentage of income or net worth. Please keep in mind that these are only guidelines. A number of additional factors, like past giving history, timing, the donor's ability to replace assets, etc., should be considered in addition to the donor's financial ability.

Gift Request To Be Given Over Time	Based On Minimum Income	Minimum Assets
$ 10,000	$ 50,000	$ 200,000
$ 25,000	$ 100,000	$ 500,000
$ 50,000	$ 250,000	$ 500,000
$ 100,000	$ 250,000	$ 1,000,000
$ 500,000	$ 500,000	$ 5,000,000
$ 1,000,000	$ 500,000	$ 10,000,000

Rule of Thumb #2:

During a campaign, generally it will take at least three qualified prospects for each single gift you hope to secure at each giving level.

Sample Prospect Potential Report

5 Year Capability	Existing Constituency	Cumulative Capability	Proposed Campaign Goal	Gifts Required	Total Prospects Needed (3:1 Ratio)	Prospect Balance Needed
$1,000,000+	2	$2,000,000	$2,000,000	2	6	4
$500,000-999,999	7	$3,500,000	$3,000,000	6	18	11
$250,000-499,999	12	$3,000,000	$3,000,000	9	27	15
$100,000-249,999	21	$2,100,000	$2,500,000	25	75	54
$50,000-99,999	47	$2,350,000	$2,500,000	50	150	103
$25,000-49,999	110	$2,750,000	$2,500,000	100	300	190
$10,000-24,999	182	$1,820,000	$2,000,000	200	600	418
$5,000-9,999	300	$1,500,000	$1,500,000	300	900	600
$1,000-4,999	1,750	$1,750,000	$1,000,000	1,000	3,000	1,250
Total	**2,431**	**$20,770,000**	**$20,000,000**	**1,692**	**5,076**	**2,645**

Have you conducted a pre-campaign inventory for your organization? Use the following grid to identify top priority needs—in each category—at your institution.

Major Gifts Grid			
GIFT RANGE	PEOPLE	PROGRAMS	FACILITIES
$25,000			
$50,000			
$100,000			
$500,000			
$1 MILLION			

22

Keep an Eye on the Prize

$\mathbf{A}$ Scale of Gifts model is an important way to maintain focus throughout the duration of a major campaign. Whether attempting to raise $500,000 or $5 million, the Scale of Gifts model helps illustrate both the number and size of gifts needed to achieve campaign success. It also helps in evaluating campaign success throughout the solicitation period.

Although a thorough campaign assessment will provide the basis for a Scale of Gifts model, basic questions need to be answered in order to customize a model that addresses an organization's particular circumstances:

1. What is a challenging, yet attainable goal for the nonprofit?

2. Who will be solicited? All donors who can contribute at any level, or only donors capable of giving at a certain level?

3. What is the size of the existing prospect pool?

4. How much has been raised in previous campaigns? What were the largest gifts, and how many participated at each level of giving?

Once these questions have been addressed, begin designing a customized model. In doing so, however, keep the following two principles in mind: 1) at least 80 percent of the goal will come from less than 20 percent of the prospect pool, and 2) on average, three prospect solicitations are needed for each successful call (within each gift range).

Design two or three model alternatives and discuss them with those most intimately involved with the campaign. Once a model has been agreed upon, stick to it. Keep the model constantly before everyone involved in soliciting gifts. This model can be used as an ongoing tool in focusing on gifts needed in each category to achieve campaign success.

Scale of Gifts Needed to Secure $5 Million Based on 100 Gifts of $10,000 and Above

Prospects Gift Range	Prospects Needed	Gifts Needed	Amount
$1,000,000	3	1	$ 1,000,000
$500,000 - 999,999	6	2	$ 1,000,000
$250,000 - 499,000	12	4	$ 1,000,000
$100,000 - 249,999	15	5	$ 500,000
$50,000 - 99,999	30	10	$ 500,000
$25,000 - 49,999	60	20	$ 500,000
$10,000 - 24,999	150	50	$ 500,000
	276	92	$ 5,000,000

Scale of Gifts Needed to Secure $5 Million
Based on 1,800 Gifts of $500 and Above

Prospects Gift Range	Prospects Needed	Gifts Needed	Amount
$500,000	3	1	$ 500,000
$250,000-499,000	6	2	$ 500,000
$100,000-249,999	12	4	$ 400,000
$75,000-99,999	21	7	$ 525,000
$50,000-74,999	27	9	$ 450,000
$25,000-49,999	45	15	$ 375,000
$10,000-24,999	75	25	$ 250,000
$5,000-9,999	300	100	$ 500,000
$2,500-4,999	600	200	$ 500,000
$1,000-2,499	1,500	500	$ 500,000
$500-999	3,000	1,000	$ 500,000
	5,589	1,863	$5,000,000

23

Match Prospects' Interests with Projects

$\mathbf{O}$nce lead gifts have been solicited during a campaign and the public phase begins, how are new sources for potential gifts identified?

The College of Wooster incorporated an "interest card" as a means of identifying and matching prospects with campaign projects.

According to Sara Patton, vice president for development at Wooster, "We wanted to avoid sending pledge cards out before our volunteers could make personal calls on key prospects, so we decided to use a response form that helped match individuals' interests with our campaign projects."

A letter and interest card were mailed to some 25,000 alumni, parents, and friends of the institution with about 1.5 percent (300 to 500) responding. Those responding were sent additional information that provided details on the campaign project(s) where they expressed interest. If, for instance, an individual returned the interest card indicating an interest in the new library, additional information was sent to the prospect including floor plans and gift opportunities available for that project. At that point, a development officer or volunteer would follow up with a personal visit to the prospect.

Patton says the interest card served as an effective way of identifying new prospects for the campaign.

Wooster's Campaign for the 1990s, with an original goal of $65 million, concluded in June 1996, and raised $75.3 million.

Campaign Interest Card (Side One)

Wooster's Campaign for the 1990s
The College of Wooster

DECISION MAKING INFORMATION

This is not a pledge card.

What is the scope and purpose of the projects to be funded by the campaign?
We have prepared detailed information describing what the scope and purpose is for each subject within the campaign categories of capital projects, endowment needs, and operating funds.

How to give to the campaign:
We have also prepared information answering the most frequently asked questions about how to give to the campaign.

Please review the list on the back and check off the subjects of most interest to you.

The College will send you the information you have requested for your consideration.

Campaign Interest Card (Side Two)

I WOULD LIKE TO KNOW MORE ABOUT THE
FOLLOWING:

Capital Projects
- ❏ New Library
- ❏ Science Library in Frick Hall
- ❏ Art Center
- ❏ Severance Chemistry Building

Endowment Needs
- ❏ Professorships
- ❏ Scholarships
- ❏ Independent Study
- ❏ Office of the Chaplain
- ❏ Library Funds

Operating Funds
- ❏ The Wooster Fund
- ❏ Scholarship Funds

How to Make a Gift to the Campaign
- ❏ Cash
- ❏ Pledges
- ❏ Appreciated Securities
- ❏ Life Income Options
- ❏ Estate Commitments

PLEASE PRINT
Name_____
Street Address_____
City State Zip Code_____
Day Phone Evening Phone_____

24

Don't Let Prospects Fall Through the Cracks

While attending a luncheon, a fund raiser is passed a slip of paper with the name of a prospect requiring cultivation. In the midst of a busy fund-raising schedule, time never materializes to follow up on the new prospect. Another potential donor has just fallen through the cracks.

Sound familiar? All too often and for a number of reasons—everything from "he won't return my phone calls" to "if I could get out of some of these meetings, I could begin calling on my prospects"—prospect cultivation and solicitation get pushed to the bottom of the pile.

The Active Prospect Management Report is a tool that helps fund raisers stay focused on prospects who need continued cultivation or solicitation. It helps fund raisers visualize the process of bringing each prospect closer to the realization of a major gift over a specified period of time. The report is particularly helpful when managing a large group of prospects (i.e., campaign or planned gift lists), for a project or program.

The report should be completed once a month. It provides: 1) an ongoing record of activities that have taken place with each prospect, and 2) a clear picture of what needs to occur with each prospect over the next 30 days.

Feel free to design a prospect management report that best fits the personality of your organization or use the model as a way to get started.

Here are some tips for using this report:

- **Solicitor's initials.** This is the person responsible for eventually soliciting the gift. It may be a staff member or volunteer.

95

- **Manager's initials.** This is the person responsible for managing the ongoing identification, research, cultivation, solicitation, and stewardship of the prospect pool. The prospect manager may or may not be the solicitor.

- **Prospect's name.** This simply refers to the name of the prospect.

- **Prospect's region.** This is used depending on the geographic size of the prospect pool. Or substitute another criteria such as "gift type" or "prospect constituency."

- **Likelihood of a gift (P-F-G-E).** These criteria represent a judgment call. In other words, what are the odds of getting a gift? P = poor, F = fair, G = good, and E = excellent. Forcing a decision on the likelihood of a gift every 30 days helps prioritize the amount of attention a prospect should be receiving.

- **Gift size.** Refers to the size of gift sought from the prospect.

- **Movement.** Refers to the amount of activity that has taken place with the prospect in the past 30 days. [0] refers to no activity, [-] refers to negative activity and [+] refers to positive activity. For instance, no contact or communication with the prospect would mean a [0] in that category. On the other hand, if the prospect was irritated by something the organization did, list a [-] for negative movement in the past 30 days.

Rules of Thumb

Keep in mind that the following information is not "hard and fast," but meant to be used as a guideline in estimating an individual's ability to give:

- A potential major gift might be calculated by multiplying the rate of an individual's consistent giving by 20.

- An appropriate major gift may be equal to 5 percent of a donor's known assets.

- One way to estimate an individual's net worth is by multiplying his or her current salary by 10.

- One estimate of giving ability is equal to 10 percent of stock and option holdings worth $1 million or more.

- **Personal time and effort.** How much measurable time and/or effort has been devoted to the cultivation or solicitation of this prospect in the last 30 days? Simply list the amount of time in terms of hours or portion of an hour.

- **Months needed for decision.** How many months will it take to receive an answer on whether or not the prospect will contribute to the program? In some cases, it may take less than one month. In other instances, it may take as long as 24 months.

- **Personal time and effort.** Refers to the amount of time to be devoted to the prospect during the next 30 days.

- **Type of next contact.** Will this mean phoning the prospect, drafting a proposal directed to the prospect, or meeting face-to-face with the prospect? Once again, the criteria help to prioritize the plan in bringing the prospect closer to the realization of a gift.

- **Comments.** This category provides an opportunity to list special circumstances specific to that prospect. They may pertain to the past 30 days or the next 30 days.

Why Have a Quiet Phase?

- The pre-campaign phase allows quiet, private solicitation for major gifts. This lets major gift prospects know they are on the inside and their commitments will play a role in setting the final campaign goal.

- Success with major lead gifts will help determine whether or not the campaign goal is in line with earlier predictions. Prematurely announcing a campaign could place the campaign in the difficult situation of decreasing or failing to meet a goal once it has been set.

Active Prospect Management Report

Completed By _____

Month/Year _____

Solicitor	Manager	Prospect	Region	Likelihood of Gift	Gift Size	Last Thirty Days			Next Thirty Days		Comments
						Movement [0 - +]	Personal Time	Months for Decision	Personal Time	Type of Next Contact	

New Prospect Considerations Report

NAME	REFERRED BY	REFERRAL DATE	ASSIGNED TO	RATIONALE FOR CONSIDERATION	ACTION TAKEN	BY

When you secure new names, or referrals are given to you, record them on a New Prospect Considerations Report that calls for action to be taken within a specific time frame with clear objectives in mind.

Board Involvement & Qualifications

25

Elements of Quality Board Members

What qualities are most important when considering new board members? Should they be familiar with the organization? Should they be current donors?

Although there will always be exceptions, here are some important characteristics to consider when enlisting capable board members:

- Belief in the mission

- Ability to separate policy from management issues

- Affluence

- Influence

- Previous gifts to the agency

- Meeting attendance

- Meets organization's gender, minority or other goals

- Track record on other boards

- Ability to get things done

- Brings unique talent to the board

- Willingness to become involved in fund development

- Respected by others
- Ability to enlist and motivate
- Can be counted on to follow through on projects
- Compatible with other board members and CEO

No matter how urgent the need or worthy the cause, a campaign is lifeless until those closest to the organization lend it legs and give it a voice. Board members must realize that without their active participation in identification, cultivation, and solicitation of peers that can advance the organization's mission, a campaign is just potential energy. Active, motivated board members can transform potential into a potent campaign.

26

Is the Organization Recruiting Good Board Members ... or Just Dead Wood?

Administrators of nonprofits know the more successful a person is, the more likely it is he or she will be asked to serve as a member of a board of directors. This is a fact. However, just because someone is a successful business person does not necessarily mean he or she will be a successful board member.

Presidents, executive directors, and others who are responsible for colleges, universities, hospitals, museums, youth centers, clubs, social service agencies and other nonprofits are looking for successful and well-known community people to serve on their boards. They know to look for people in the community, such as bankers, attorneys, corporate CEOs, small business leaders, locally elected officials, hospital CEOs, doctors, etc., being sure to build a board representing the diversity of community talent.

But, are these individuals board material? Can just anyone serve on a board of directors? Or are special skills needed? These questions must be answered before asking the person to serve, not after.

When an appointment is made to visit with a candidate about the agency, be prepared to fully inform him or her about what is expected. Provide any written policies pertaining to board members. At some point during the meeting, address the following:

1) **What are the agency's mission, history and programs.** Explain in detail.

2) **How long is the term of service?** If the institution does not have set term limits, be very careful. The person recruited may become a lifetime member of the "Dead Wood Society." If there are already several of these "lifers" on the board, not much will be accomplished unless they are willing to work in the new millennium.

3) **How much time is required?** Successful people did not become successful by sitting around doing nothing. They are busy and can spare little time. They should be given specific and precise meeting times and places (i.e., the third Tuesday of each month from 5 - 7 p.m. in the boardroom). The recruit must be willing to set aside these times. If board members are expected to be at the monthly fund-raising event, the prospect should be informed of this as well. If the annual meeting is an all day affair they need to know about it. And, if the agency plans an all day strategic planning retreat the second Saturday in June, for example, this also needs to be conveyed. Even though this information is presented to the board prospect, there are still some people who will join a board, but seldom show for meetings—offering the excuse, "the time does not work with my schedule."

4) **Who else is on the board?** This should not be an issue, but there are occasions when an agency enlists new people to the board only to find several members do not see eye-to-eye on much of anything. This makes for a very uncomfortable situation for everyone and should be avoided. Instead, the person approaching a prospective board member should present a current board list.

5) **What is the overall status of the institution, including financial, public image, and so on?** Most people are not eager to volunteer their time, talent and treasures to an agency if it is one step away from bankruptcy or if the agency's "dirty laundry" has been aired in the daily news. However, if there is a strategic plan for addressing and improving these issues, it should be covered with the board prospect.

6) **Is this an advisory committee or board of directors?** Some agencies have advisory committees that act as a board of directors, but the difference is they have little, if any power. They are to advise, not direct. Board prospects should be well aware of their roles. Advisory board members have been known to quit attending meetings because they do not feel their votes count, or they mistakenly thought they had more power.

7) **Is a major fund-raising event or campaign currently being planned or discussed?** If prospects are walking into the middle of a major campaign, they may not wish to join the board at this time. There are mixed feelings whether it is wise to bring on new board members during a campaign. Prospects should be fully informed of the upcoming event or campaign and told what their responsibilities will be. Then, if they decide to join, they are aware of their role.

8) **How involved is the board in raising funds for the institution?** The board's role in fund raising has already been discussed to some extent, but there is a purpose for rephrasing this question. It is one thing to be told the board is responsible for a fund-raising event each year in October. It is something entirely different when, in September, the board is asked to give a list of their friends and colleagues who could contribute $1,000 to the agency. Some board members feel uncomfortable asking friends for $1,000. Under these circumstances an agency may be unable to secure many interested and influential people for the board.

9) **Are board members required to contribute a certain amount each year to the agency?** While it is common for board members to contribute to the agency they serve, it should be conveyed if there is a specific dollar amount expected. Some agencies expect board members to contribute $1,000 per year, and some even more. Expect prospective board members to inquire about the details of this policy.

10) **Is the executive director the only staff member who reports directly to the board?** Is there a "chain of command" policy for the staff to follow? Situations sometimes arise when staff members feel they cannot go to the executive director with a problem. Instead, they go directly to one of the board members. This causes distress for everyone concerned. If there is a policy in place that states the chain of command, the singled out board member can refer the staff member back to the policy.

11) **Does the institution have a list of committees with assigned board members?** This list, with a full explanation of duties, should be presented to the board prospect. If these committee assignments require time other than what was stated as board time, the prospect should be made aware of the assignment. When reviewing the committee list, board prospects should be asked if they have an area of interest or whether they would like to serve on a specific committee.

Nothing is more frustrating for the head of an agency than working with board members who are "dead wood." They seldom attend meetings. They often cancel at the last minute a catered luncheon meeting. A nonprofit does not have money to throw away on uneaten meals.) They may only attend every other meeting, then expect everyone to wait while the events of the last meeting are explained. They seldom, if ever, attend fund-raising events, leaving the work to other members of the board. (The 80/20 principle really shines here. Twenty percent of the people do eighty percent of the work.)

Serving as the director of an institution can be very fulfilling—a lot of work, but very fulfilling. However, having the right mix of people guiding the group can make the work of the director much easier. When the board is well versed in its responsibilities and takes those responsibilities seriously, things run smoothly. By preparing prospective board members with what they can expect, the nonprofit organization can expect less "dead wood" and more, "Yes, I would!"

27

What Qualifies a Board for Campaign Success?

Knowing that the board will play a critical role in a campaign's success, and getting members to recognize that, is a major accomplishment. What characteristics will manifest themselves among the campaign-ready board?

These characteristics describe a board committed to campaign success. Members:

- own the strategic plan because they helped design it.

- are prepared to make their own sacrificial leadership gifts first.

- have major gift solicitation experience.

- willingly attend campaign meetings and make solicitation calls.

- recognize successful campaigns are elitist, not populist.

- inspire one another.

- make realistic commitments of time and knowledge.

- grasp the quiet phase strategy of a major campaign.

- understand the bulk of support will come from individuals, not corporations.

- are committed to the campaign and to recruiting others to help.

107

Unfortunately there is no perfect, front-end assessment to determine who will make a great board member and who will not. Past performance, however, can be a good indicator of future achievements. In addition, the synergy of members working for a common cause can multiply enthusiasm and productivity.

The time and effort invested in securing and equipping board members is a long-term enterprise, but it offers the possibility of great returns.

Campaign Leadership & Organization

28

In Search of C.I.V.I.C. Leadership

What characteristics should organizations look for when building a volunteer corps, structuring a board, or searching out prospects that might help financially on a project or in a campaign? The answer to each search is the same—boiled down to five areas forming the acronym C.I.V.I.C. The following is a checklist of characteristics to look for when searching for C.I.V.I.C. leadership.

Capacity.

Capacity comes in many forms. A prospect may have the capacity of time necessary to give service to the organization, the financial capacity to assist the organization to fund its mission, or hopefully a combination of both. Capacity is a matter of having the resources that target the organization's needs. Many types of resources may be necessary to fulfill many needs at many levels.

Knowing what capacity means is easy, but analyzing capacity is an imprecise process. Some people can "hear the money," but many others use subjective means. One approach is a traditional method: by speaking directly with prospects and visiting with their friends and associates. These meetings become cultivation builders, as well as information-gathering opportunities. In the broadest application, such as the development of prospect lists, use screening sessions to invite a representative cross-section of current volunteers and donors to discuss names on a list.

Another sense of capacity may be gained through technical research into public records. The former process is usually more effective because one-on-one discussions give individuals the opportunity to reveal their capacity—which removes some of the guesswork.

Interest.

Capacity without an interest in the organization leads to very few positive results. On the other hand, an extremely strong interest level will lead an individual to stretch his or her support of a project. If Bill Gates knows nothing about a project going on 2,000 miles away, he is not a prospect for the campaign. (He often shows up on prospect lists for no other reason than his immense wealth and somebody's guess that he ought to find the organization's mission interesting.) The retired teacher who never married, however, may leave his entire estate to support a program for educating the disadvantaged in a particular city. In short, the formula "capacity + interest = gift" expresses the dynamic between these first two characteristics of C.I.V.I.C. leadership. It also stands to reason that if two individuals have roughly the same capacity, the one with the greatest interest will make the larger gift.

Cultivation, education, and involvement are the best steps to take toward increasing interest. This work may begin on any level, depending upon the nature of the relationship with the prospect. There is nothing wrong with starting the process by simply contacting the individual for the first time and asking for the opportunity to visit with him or her about the organization. If this is impossible on a one-to-one basis, try a small group gathering held in a neutral location. Volunteers and philanthropists are genuinely interested in knowing what is going on in their communities, and cultivation of their interest should start with this assumption.

Visibility.

The visibility of the organization is related directly to the visibility of associated individuals. Even when an organization happens to be a household word—The Salvation Army, for example—people associated with the organization still create its visibility when it comes down to the local community level. Despite the fact that year after year The Army raises more funds than any other nationally based not-for-profit, there are some communities where The Army board is not well known. In these areas The Army has no advantage over other similar not-for-profits, and may even be disadvantaged.

The stock of the organization goes up when visible people sign on to help, and the organization's credibility increases. This is why, for example, the boards of Planned Parenthood almost always include leading ministers or rabbis from the community. Look for highly visible people who may have a natural affinity for the cause, and place them under cultivation.

Influence.

"People give to people, not to cancer," a saying goes. It is certainly true that the growth of an organization, its visibility, or its success at raising funds is related directly to the strength of its interpersonal relationships. Associating with people of influence in the community is one of the key strategies necessary in order to "grow" the organization. The same strategies apply to involving people with influence as those employed with people with visibility. In both cases the process is about informing and involving people before asking them to invest.

Commitment.

The final characteristic represented by the acronym C.I.V.I.C. is commitment. Having supporters with commitment is the end goal of all cultivation. Once commitment is achieved, the "gift" follows. Volunteers work harder and donors give more when they are fully committed to the organization and its mission.

Commitment follows interest, and it leverages capacity. Commitment is contagious. A few committed volunteers and donors can spark whole groups of people into action, and make the difference between the success and failure of a fund drive or campaign. Committed people are the best advocates and advertisement an organization can have.

Each of these characteristics must be present in the members of the ideal leadership team. Although the best situation exists when every member embodies all of these characteristics, in reality organizations should hope for and seek a blend. Since each characteristic attracts its own kind, the blending of these traits among volunteers and donors creates a vitality that enlarges and self-perpetuates the overall make-up of supporting groups. Ultimately, C.I.V.I.C. leadership secures an organization's ability to fulfill its mission.

29

Steering Committee Leads to Success

A campaign steering committee's structure is nearly as individual as campaigns. However, all steering committees share some similarities and have some common concerns.

Who will serve on the steering committee depends on the focus of the campaign. Patricia Szuch, director of capital giving at Ball State University, Muncie, Indiana, says they based their selections in part on where graduates live, since the campaign targeted that constituency. Her central executive committee for a $7.5 million campaign, which concluded in December 1997, consisted of 12 people. This served as a core for this campaign and future efforts. The core group represented most of the targeted geographic areas. The development staff then screened other alumni and presented those names to the core committee for consideration on the 100-member steering committee.

"We started out thinking our steering committee would be about 50 people, but decided it needed to be larger to have groups of volunteers to represent all areas where our alumni are located. The entire group was involved from the start of the campaign in December 1993. The core group met quarterly for the first couple of years and the entire steering committee met annually," Szuch says.

The work required that all members return to campus for planning during the early portion of the campaign. After public announcement of the campaign, development staff traveled to committee members' locations for meetings and presentations involving prospective donors. Committee members were responsible for screening lists of prospects in their area, then setting up meetings between donors and staff.

Consideration for selection was based on developing a team that represented Ball State's 75-year history. Both gender and race were deemed important as well as community volunteers from all walks of life. Commitment to the university as a student and alumnus, as well as financial potential was also important. "Financial criteria was important since between 25 and 33 percent of funds for the campaign came from committee members," notes Szuch. They also act as spokespersons and are asked to be present at area campaign meetings.

Committee's Work Begins Long Before a Public Announcement

All committees should be established early in the campaign process, definitely prior to any public announcement about the campaign. "The group's hardest and most intensive work takes place then," says Carla M. Cooper, currently senior vice president for health care philanthropy at St. Luke's Episcopal Hospital in Houston, and formerly associate vice chancellor for institutional advancement with the University of Houston System. "At the beginning, the committee members struggle to clarify what they are doing and why, and who will help them do it. Then the focus shifts to the tremendously complex communications involved in tracking prospect relationships. Leadership must agree upon a case with a reasonable sense of goal—one that is feasible and documented by analysis."

Committee size also is variable and depends on the size of the campaign and how much responsibility committee members will have. "It could be two, five, or ten people. Steering committee members carry the campaign as far as prospect cultivation and solicitation. In large part, they identify a core group of volunteers and then focus on major gift solicitations," Cooper says.

The size of the campaign and its structure are designed to represent key organization components that will determine the committee size and its composition. The committee needs to have a balance of people skilled in raising capital and those who are visibly compelling in the community. Committees usually remain intact throughout the life of the campaign.

"The committee must remember to maintain good communication with members of the institution's staff," Cooper says. "There has to be a really good working relationship to keep track of all communications between committee members and prospects."

Communication no longer means that all committee members must be physically present for frequently held meetings. "Now there are technologies like teleconference, e-mail, and so on. The challenge can be to use those alternative means of communication," Cooper says.

Designation of a committee chairperson may depend on the number of persons or campaign components involved. If there are several key components to the campaign, people representing those interests might serve together as a committee core under the guidance of one person in a position of overall institution leadership.

Limit the Size of the Core Steering Committee

Review of how the steering committee performed can be helpful before it is time to establish another. John R. Chandler, special assistant to the headmaster at The Hotchkiss School in Lakeville, Connecticut, says a committee will be more effective if it is not too large. "The steering committee has a life of its own that changes over the course of the campaign. We started with six or seven members but at one time had as many as 20. It became unwieldy and communication was difficult. Then we reduced it to eight or nine again, including the people who did the lion's share of strategizing and solicitation. The committee should be flexible, possibly with a secondary component such as a council of advisors who are also involved but not in all the major decisions."

Chandler says the choice for committee chairperson is not always immediately evident. He first solicited a person who was a good leader, but did not want the job. Chandler's friend told him not to worry—to find seven or eight people to get the committee's work under way, and that the right chairperson would "rise to the top" of that group. "I got people of a variety of ages, and sure enough, the right person did come to the top and was chairperson for the first three years of the campaign. That committee was able to set the parameters for the campaign," which started out with a goal of $40 million that was raised to $100 million two years later. The campaign eventually surpassed its goal, raising about $103 million.

Chandler's support role was primarily maintaining constant contact with the committee members and keeping them informed about his solicitation activities. He also helped arrange meetings with prospective large donors and key members of the school's administrators and leaders. "I sort of became a field general," Chandler says.

Encouraging committee members to follow through with their responsibilities can be difficult. "You have to be understanding of a volunteer's schedule, but there comes a time when you have to reassign prospects. Learn whom to count on. It's important that you keep the lines of communication open with key volunteers and begin to bypass those you can't count on. It's OK to ease them out if necessary," Chandler says.

Guidelines for Building an
Effective Steering Committee

- Establish committees early in the campaign process.

- Determine committee size by the magnitude of the campaign.

- Keep the group small enough to prevent it from being unwieldy and adversely impacting effective communication.

- Balance money-raising skills and positive constituency visibility in committee membership.

- Make sure all facets of the organization are represented on the committee.

- Consider the giving potential of committee members.

- Choose committee members who have demonstrated participation as volunteers.

- Keep communication lines open between committee members and paid institution staff.

- Designate one effective leader to guide the group as a whole.

- Encourage committee members to follow through on assignments.

- Ease out ineffective committee members and volunteers.

- Evaluate the committee's effectiveness after the campaign's end.

Campaign Organization Summaries

Ball State University
Campaign Goal . . . .$7.5 million
Campaign Duration . . . . .Dec. 1993 - Dec. 1997
Amount Raised . . . .$5.7 million
Steering Committee Size . . . . .100 members
Committee Responsibility . . . . .Demonstrate commitment by
          pledging
          Recruit other steering committee
          members
          Open doors with prospects
          Screen geographic area rosters
          Host events
          Go on personal calls

The Hotchkiss School
Campaign Goal . . . .$100 million
Campaign Duration . . . . .1989 - Dec. 1995
Amount Raised . . . .$103 million
Steering Committee Size . . . . .8 to 10 members
Committee Responsibility . . . . .Make calls
          Establish and monitor campaign
          guidelines

University of Houston System
Campaign Goal . . . .$350 million
Campaign Duration . . . . .Six years
Amount Raised . . . .$358 million
Steering Committee Size . . . . .12 members
Committee Responsibility . . . . .Establish goals
          Determine policies
          Approve plan and calendar
          General advocacy

30

A Time Line is a Plan

A Time Line is essential to the preparation and progress of any organization's fund-raising efforts. More than a calendar of events, a well-planned Time Line is an indispensable map that outlines the path of predetermined goals that add up to success. A Time Line reflects all the important milestones established by an agency in order to help maintain, for staff and volunteers, a common vision and coordinated implementation.

The Time Line indicates the function of various donors, volunteers and staff positions and shows when certain tasks should be performed. Donor identification, cultivation, qualification, and solicitation are mapped out in sequence. The Time Line lists the modes of communication to be utilized—written and oral, private and public. A complete Time Line even delineates policies that must be developed and indicates when this will be accomplished.

A Time Line reveals what still needs to be done and when. Because staff members and volunteers are able to see the sequence of tasks, they can be unified in their efforts and more realistic in their expectations.

On the following two pages is an example of a two-year campaign Time Line. The importance is the illustration of time parameters.

The following is an example of a two year campaign time line. The importance is the illustration of time parameters.

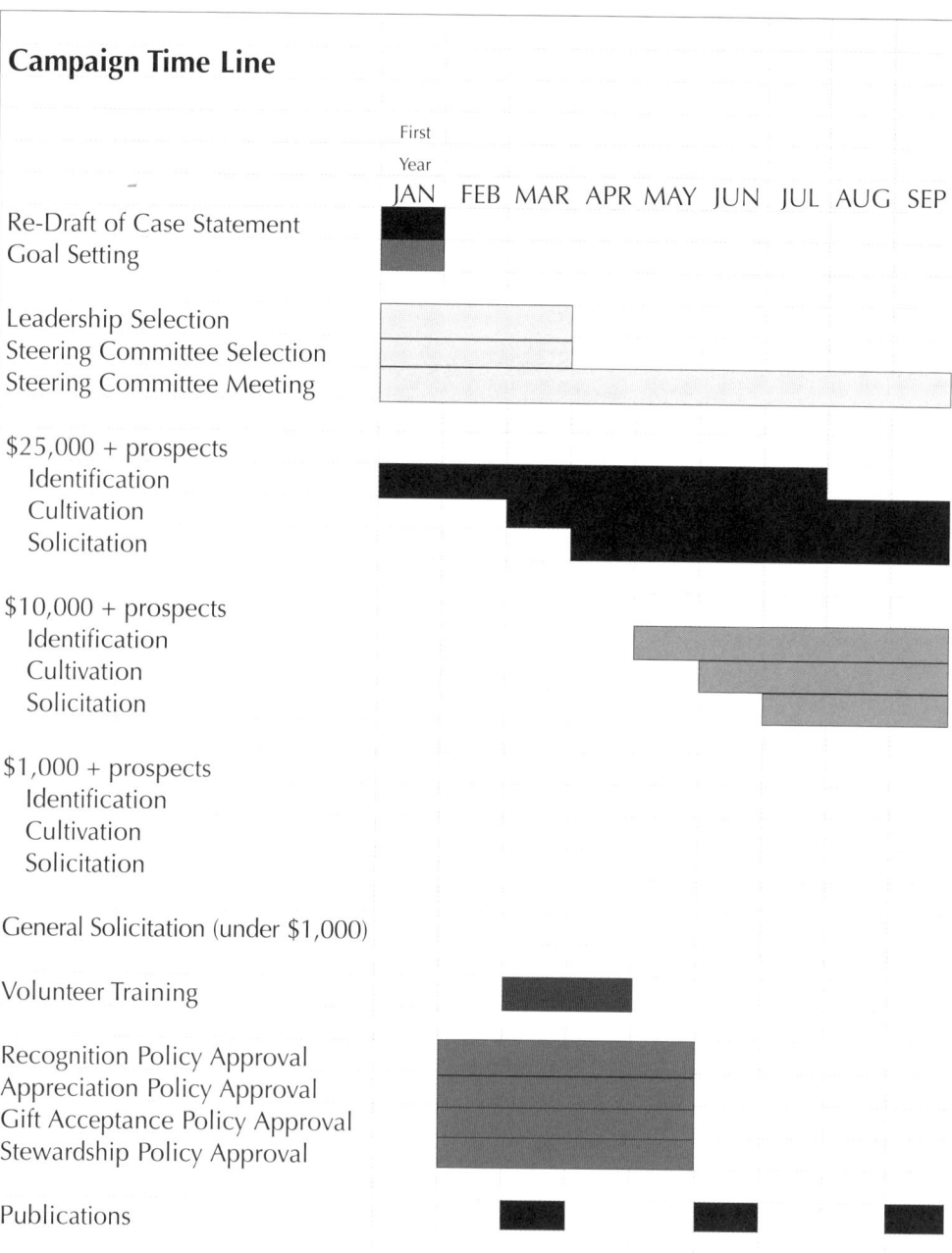

Campaign Time Line

	First Year								
	JAN	FEB	MAR	APR	MAY	JUN	JUL	AUG	SEP

Re-Draft of Case Statement
Goal Setting

Leadership Selection
Steering Committee Selection
Steering Committee Meeting

$25,000 + prospects
  Identification
  Cultivation
  Solicitation

$10,000 + prospects
  Identification
  Cultivation
  Solicitation

$1,000 + prospects
  Identification
  Cultivation
  Solicitation

General Solicitation (under $1,000)

Volunteer Training

Recognition Policy Approval
Appreciation Policy Approval
Gift Acceptance Policy Approval
Stewardship Policy Approval

Publications

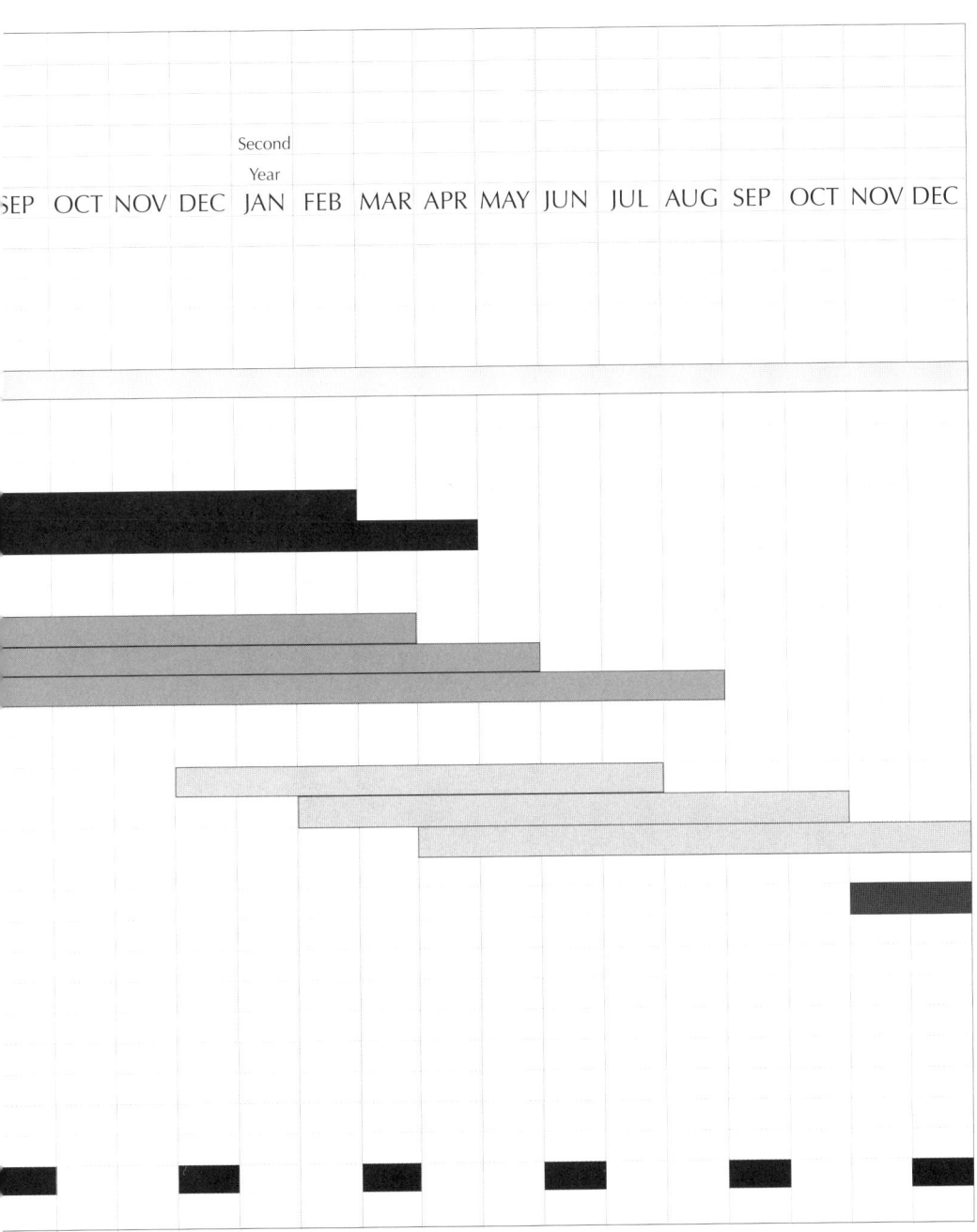

	SEP	OCT	NOV	DEC	Second Year JAN	FEB	MAR	APR	MAY	JUN	JUL	AUG	SEP	OCT	NOV	DEC

In order to broaden the base of ownership in the organization's mission, a streamlined and efficient organization should be structured to include leadership beyond the board. Typically, campaign organizations, especially the steering committee, are ad hoc groups who come together for the purpose of providing leadership to the campaign and frequently continue to engage in the life of the organization after the campaign is complete. A typical Campaign Organizational Chart is shown on the opposite page.

CAMPAIGN ORGANIZATIONAL CHART

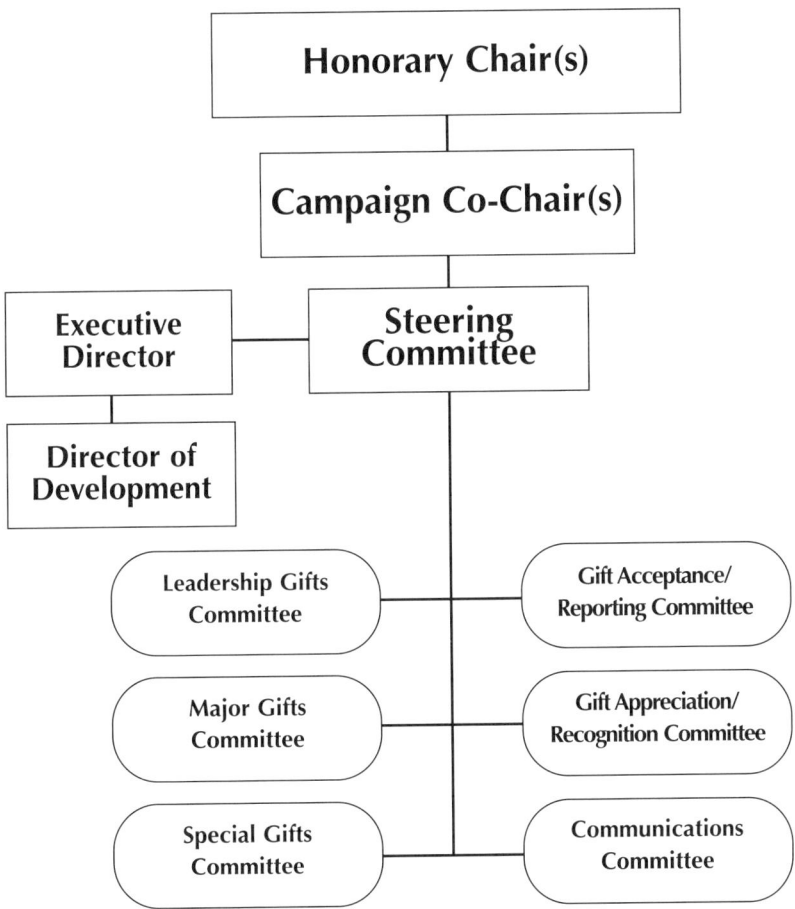

Campaign Cultivation & Solicitation

31

Cultivate Major Donor Prospects

How can the ongoing cultivation of individual prospects be monitored?

The Individual Prospect Management Form is helpful in doing just that—planning and monitoring the systematic cultivation of major gift prospects.

Although estimates vary among consultants, a single fund raiser can manage the cultivation of 100 prospects assuming he or she spends 80 percent of his or her time in major gift cultivation. (When spending less time in major gift cultivation, decrease the number managed throughout a year.)

Assuming once again that each prospect should receive an average of eight cultivation "moves" each year toward the realization of a major gift commitment, it becomes important to have a manageable way of monitoring those cultivation "moves." This may be as simple as a birthday card or as time-consuming as a joint fishing trip.

Maintaining a notebook of Individual Prospect Management Forms can help in following a planned cultivation schedule and ensure that each prospect is receiving the attention required to realize a major gift.

Whether it is a phone call, written correspondence or an interview for an article in a magazine or newsletter, date all contacts with major prospects (under the appropriate category), to ensure prospects are getting the attention they deserve. Each contact should, in one way or another, strengthen the nonprofit's relationship with that prospect.

Also, be sure to list (under the "Scheduled Cultivation" category) events or programs that will serve in cultivating all prospects throughout the year.

Use the "Comments" section to highlight information that may effect future cultivation calls.

The Individual Prospect Management Form will help keep things focused on those who can give the most.

INDIVIDUAL PROSPECT MANAGEMENT FORM
Hillcrest Family Services

Prospect: _____ Title: _____
Spouse: _____ Business: _____
Address: _____ Business Address:_____
City/State/Zip: _____ City/State/Zip: _____
(H) Phone: _____ (W) Phone: _____

	LETTER	PHONE	PERSONAL VISIT	SCHEDULED CULTIVATION	COMMENTS
JAN					
FEB					
MARCH					
APRIL					
MAY					
JUNE					
JULY					
AUG					
SEPT					
OCT					
NOV					
DEC					

INDIVIDUAL CULTIVATION PLAN
St. Joseph Healthcare Foundation

Name: _____ Date: _____

Address: _____ Phone: _____

Prospect Manager: _____

Staff Assigned: _____

Volunteer Assigned: _____

Anticipated Solicitor(s): _____

Target Solicitation Date: _____ Target Amount: _____

Possible Use of Funds

1. _____ 4. _____

2. _____ 5. _____

3. _____ 6. _____

DATE	ANTICIPATED MOVE	BY WHOM	OUTCOME

Points of Interest:

Developing a cultivation plan for each prospect will help in moving the prospect closer to the realization of a major gift, and will also help to better manage the cultivation of several major gift prospects over a period of time.

32

"Terrific Tuesdays" Acquaint Prospects With Needs

When the Boys & Girls Clubs of the Lowcountry in South Carolina needed a boost in a campaign, staff members initiated a Terrific Tuesdays program where small groups of prospects toured the current facility to get a better idea why the campaign was needed.

Kay E. Merrill, director of development, says the program was very successful. The campaign began in May 1996 with a goal of $5.5 million to plan, build, equip, and endow a new 27,000-square-foot Boys & Girls Club. Ground was broken in October 1997 with pledges, at that time, of more than $5.8 million. In the end, more than $6 million had been raised.

"The tour program served to educate potential donors," Merrill said. "We personally invited not more than 12 people each week to attend a Terrific Tuesday. At least one board member and spouse, along with one or two staff members, served as hosts. Guests were offered refreshments, shown our campaign video, given an overview of the project, and a tour."

After the tour, guests invariably commented that they previously had no idea what the clubs were providing and that, thanks to the special tour, they realized there was an obvious need for a new facility.

Handwritten thank-yous followed the tours, along with follow-up visits.

Merrill says every Terrific Tuesday tour resulted in a donation. One gift was for $250,000 and another was $100,000—both from people who were not previous donors. The program also resulted in new volunteers for the clubs.

33

Brief the Solicitation Team

When inviting others to join in the solicitation of a major gift, spend time briefing and training the team members before the solicitation.

- Talk about the questions or issues that might be raised by the prospect and try to anticipate who will respond and what that response will be.

- Role-play the solicitation. Practice asking for the gift. Speaking words out loud and hearing how they sound will help shape and refine the request for support.

- Plan the exit. Know in advance when to conclude the conversation.

In addition, know that when the commitment to contribute has been made, it does not stop there. How will the gift be paid? Over what period of time? Does the donor wish to be reminded of payments when they are due? This is the time to secure closure on all questions relating to the gift.

34

Guide for the Successful Campaign Solicitor

Steering committee members make an honorable commitment to improve the community and the lives of their neighbors. Their role in a campaign cannot be underestimated. Their time is valuable. They have offered to serve at their own expense and to make sacrifices to their busy schedules in order to help insure the campaign is a success.

The following is a sample letter sent to steering committee members to help encourage, guide, and acquaint volunteer solicitors with the position and process involved in serving on a campaign:

Dear Mr. Jones,

You were recruited because your stature in the community lends immediate respect and credibility. Your business and social connections provide this campaign with increased visibility and distinction. These intangible contributions will, no doubt, prove to be of financial benefit to the project.

When all is said and done, perhaps you only expect a modest fare of punch and cookies shared among friends at a much deserved victory party. However, you may find the rewards more gratifying than you can imagine at the end of the effort. Above all, your reward will be the sense of accomplishment for a job well done, the camaraderie of those who under-

stand your effort and sacrifice, and the deep satisfaction that comes from helping others less fortunate.

The following are a few suggestions to help you complete your assignments to everyone's satisfaction:

1) Make your own financial contribution. You already believe in the value of the campaign. By making a financial commitment before scheduling your visits, you will put yourself in the best possible frame of mind. Generosity encourages generosity. With your financial contribution firmly established, you will be free to ask others in confidence and with genuine enthusiasm.

2) Get familiar with the case statement. Thoroughly review the case statement before each call. Be ready to answer questions and discuss the details of the project without hesitation or awkward paper shuffling. Know your prospect. Anticipate questions and be ready to respond clearly and concisely. If you feel it is appropriate, take along a staff person who can help answer specific questions. The goal is to convey the mission, the needs, and the campaign solution. Sometimes a staff member can offer a firsthand interpretation of the case statement.

3) Follow the steering committee's recommendations. Nothing makes a campaign appear more disorganized than having lone-ranger volunteers. Never conduct a call without first receiving advice and consent directly from the steering committee. If you cannot attend a meeting, make sure you find out what was discussed. Stay in touch. A successful solicitation requires many layers of good decision making. Are we soliciting the right person? Are we soliciting the right person with the right gift amount? Have we chosen the right person to solicit the right person with the right gift amount? And so on ... It is critical that solicitors cooperate with the steering committee's research and recommendations.

4) Prepare a letter that clearly states the amount requested. Keep it short and to the point, but include the requested amount in the first paragraph. Hold on to the letter until the end of the visit. Ask for the gift amount within the first 10 minutes of the call. As the meeting comes to a close,

present the letter appropriately. Include a pledge card and envelope so the donor can fill it out and hand it back.

If the prospect suggests an amount in advance of your request, and if it is not the amount in the letter, thank her and present your letter anyway, indicating the amount sought and needed. If the donor says she requires additional time to consult with a spouse, accountant, attorney, etc., ask when it would be convenient for you to get back to her for the answer. If the request is deemed "too steep," suggest the pledge be fulfilled over a three to four-year period. (Campaigns typically allow a multi-year pledge arrangement, usually not to exceed five years.) Always follow up with the donor. Do not let the pledge remain in limbo. Your diligence will convey the value and importance of the pledge.

5) *One can never overly appreciate a donor. Be sure to send a note the next day, along with a professionally prepared gift acknowledgement letter from the organization. These seemingly small gestures are essential. Campaign momentum is gained or lost by the actions and attitudes of its solicitors. Keep things moving positively.*

6) *If you don't build it, gifts won't come. Every organization has its own "field of dreams." To make these dreams a reality, each volunteer must see his or her participation as vital to the campaign's overall success. Without good planning, faithful execution, and diligent follow through, gifts will not materialize. On the other hand, when everyone does his or her part, worthy goals can be achieved and surpassed.*

As in every other sector of your life, so it is with your campaign commitments—a broken promise can destroy confidence and result in diminished relationships. If you agree to call on a prospective donor, and commit to a specific plan, please adhere to the agreement. Make the call by the designated deadline. Set up the appointment. Get prepared for the meeting and go in with confidence. As with any team effort, your performance reflects on everyone else involved. If you are unable to fulfill your promise to call on a prospect, please let the leadership group know well ahead of time.

Finally, remember that what you are doing is greatly appreciated by those who know how important your time and talents really are. No successful campaign drive is carried out apart from the efforts of a generous few. Your willingness to go to others with the message of this campaign demonstrates the stature you have achieved in this community is appropriately placed.

Solicitation Tip

When setting the stage for a major gift solicitation, suggest a specific amount up front, using a chart that identifies levels of major gifts.

Refer to the chart and tell the prospect, "Picture yourself among this group of donors."

Giving the prospect a level rather than an amount can help negotiate a major gift commitment.

35

Be a Professional, Not a Technician:

Tips on Successfully Soliciting Planned Gifts

In the past 15 years there has been unprecedented growth in individual wealth—resulting largely from several raging bulls. Planned gifts are no longer just used by large, long-established nonprofits. More and more organizations see planned gifts as a viable giving option. With more than $11.5 trillion trading generational hands between now and the end of the next decade, it is important for any serious nonprofit organization to implement a planned-giving program.

Soliciting planned gifts, however, is not the same as soliciting major or annual gifts. Some organizations see planned giving as the unmitigated domain of lawyers, accountants, and financial planners. It is not. A professional fund raiser need not be a technician. There are plenty of experts who can help take care of the details. What technicians cannot do for nonprofits is help the donor see both sides of making a gift—the tax side and the philanthropic side. The fund raiser allows the donor to see what his or her gift will accomplish in human equations.

A fund raiser should be viewed as a general professional. A technician understands the computer work of a specific part of a specific car. The professional looks at the whole vehicle and has a sense of what is needed and how each part relates to the car's overall performance. When specific questions need to be resolved, the professional can find the answers.

Some organizations are large enough to have a planned giving department. While most nonprofits do not have this luxury, locating a technician is rarely a problem. A good technician becomes an expert in a specific area. A good fund-raising professional:

1) **Watches for life-changing events.** The need for completing a will or estate plan is, in part, due to acquiring a taxable estate. Taxable estates are often a product of specific events in a person's life. In addition, these events can trigger a capacity to make a major gift. The passing of a spouse, the selling of a business, the acceptance of a golden parachute, the death of a last parent—these are all life-changing events that can bring about the need for estate planning. It is important for a fund raiser to be aware of these events and to understand their ramifications.

2) **Develops a verbal repertoire as a means of introducing the subject.** Wills and estate planning are thought of as complicated and morose topics for discussion. Saying, "Let's talk about your estate" will probably not engender donor enthusiasm. It is an easy subject to put off. Saying instead, "With a gift to our organization, we can guarantee an income stream for life" will more likely create an interest. Other suggestions: "If you have the right taxable estate and include a charity in your plans, more can be left to your heirs," or "I can give you a guaranteed-dollar pay out using a charitable gift annuity," or "A gift of a house will provide tax deductions, and you will still get to stay there as long as you want." Each is a worthy lead-in. Precise, quick, and to the point, these prepared comments and others will garner the donor's attention without overwhelming them. Very often the donor will follow up with questions or ask to set a time for further discussion.

3) **Puts it in writing and provides the donor a few more details.** After an initial discussion about planned giving, get back to the donor with some written specifics. For example, if speaking to the donor about a charitable remainder trust, based on his or her annual adjusted gross income, offer written details regarding a tax write off to be used over a six-year period. Since planned giving tools tend to appear complicated and laborious, it is necessary for the fund raiser to keep sharing information a little at a time. Keep the donor involved in the process. This is not a one-step project. Provide information in small doses.

4) **Shows donors how the plan will affirm life achievements.** Provide examples of how it has been done well. Use other donor scenarios to explain (no names or particulars, please). Planned giving deals with the totality of a donor's life work. In this way, it almost

takes on a spiritual dimension. Use planned giving to reaffirm the donor's value and life achievements.

5) **Makes it a family affair.** While confidentiality is incredibly important, it is good practice to extend an invitation to planned giving discussions to the spouse, children, extended family, even the attorney, and financial planner. Most often, the prospect will not bring in the attorney or financial planner until much later in the process. Rarely, if ever, does the prospect include children or extended family. Yet the lesson is to approach donors with an open hand. Do not give the appearance that decisions must be made under the table. Do not bring division. Donors will appreciate the offer and follow through on a limited basis. Sometimes the attorney and financial planner will prove to be more adversarial than family members. This invitation lets everyone know this is an open process.

6) **Adheres to confidentiality.** When a fund raiser works with a prospect on a planned gift, he will hear much about that donor's life—divorces, marital infidelity, adopted children, alienated siblings, abusive parents, personal finances. None of this should be shared with others. While it may be important information for putting together personalized planned gifts, it is off limits for office discussion. Garner the gift, make the best plan, then keep quiet.

7) **Treats the donor as a consumer.** Because planned giving provides a variety of different tools or products, the fund raiser should approach a planned-gift prospect as an individual customer—no cookie-cutter approach. Where a charitable remainder annuity is more beneficial for one donor, a charitable remainder trust may be better for another. By addressing the unique needs of the donor, the organization will benefit. Create a win-win plan for the organization and for the donor.

Being a professional means seeing the big picture. Serve donors by helping them know what they need. Then, when the time is right, bring in a technician to take care of the specifics.

36

Top Ten List for Successful Fund-Raising Solicitations

"Terrifying."
"To be avoided as much as possible."
"Way too complicated."

Believe it or not, these comments come from professionals in the business of development and fund raising. Fund raising is not for the "faint of constitution." But how do novice fund raisers gain, master, and assimilate these skills? How do they gain wisdom and experience? How do they break down elements of an excellent fund-raising solicitation? After all, it involves so many talents. Here are some secrets to a great solicitation:

1) **Present a professional image, one committed to the mission.** Fund raisers are living, breathing examples of servants for the public good. Be proud.

2) **Have a thorough knowledge of the proposal and the request, its ramifications and how the organization is going to pay for this project later.** Practice donors' possible rebuttal questions with a colleague. Be prepared.

3) **Adopt both a casual and formal style of presentation.** Which is best in a given situation? Check out the office and the manner of dress of the donor. Are they formal? Relaxed? Apply whichever approach is appropriate to the situation.

4) **Be sensitive to the donor's time—it is valuable.** How much is too much? What if the donor is not interested in playing the "getting to know you game?" Simply move to the ask. Do not try to engage a donor in conversation when they are obviously very preoccupied. Do not take it personally.

5) **Segue naturally into the request without appearing to be motivated only to get the money.** When should the dollar request be introduced? When it seems the small talk has subsided and the presentation is ready to go, end the presentation with the ask. Then be quiet.

6) **Talk about the proposal and then let the donor have the floor.** How much time should be spent on the proposal or in talking about the institution's history or personal experiences with the organization? Surely the donor wants to get to know the fund raiser. Yes, but do not be self-focused. There is nothing worse than an ego-centered development officer.

7) **Seek out quality mentors and advisors.** Experience is a great teacher, except fund raisers do not have the luxury of that kind of time. What to do? Listen, listen, listen. Be a sponge. Take training opportunities often.

8) **When a solicitation stalls because a potential donor keeps talking or begins to complain about the institution … listen, listen, listen.** Do not make excuses. Show interest in the donor's concerns. Volunteer to follow up with information and then do! Do not take negative comments personally. Thank the donor.

9) **Do not let a week go by without a note or a phone call.**

10) **Thank yous, goodbyes, and genuine feelings of gratitude are important.** Some say, it is often dangerous to tell people to be themselves, because sometimes that is not very attractive. Always be sincere. Take note of people toward whom others gravitate. Sincerity, kindness, and humor are values to be pursued. Learn them if they do not come naturally.

Strategies For Recognition & Appreciation

37

Honor Roll Generates New Gifts

Successfully completing the last mile of a campaign can be a real challenge. That is why it pays to have strategies in place that will generate new gifts at a meaningful level.

The Anne Arundel Medical Center in Annapolis, Maryland developed a special project to help conclude its campaign.

The "Honor Roll of Women" provided the Medical Center with a way to generate gifts of $500 and, at the same time, allow friends and employees of the facility to honor their mothers and daughters and pay special tribute to the women in their lives.

When Anne Arundel Medical Center opened its new Women's Hospital in 1995, one wall was designated as an Honor Roll of Women. For a gift of $500 anyone could recognize a special woman by having her name placed on this unique wall. Each name was silk screened on one of 16 colored panels located along the main corridor, leading from the atrium to the dining room. Windows along the other side of the corridor provided natural light.

"The wall is elegant," says Susan Vogel, manager of the foundation. "It is a beautiful place."

The project proved an excellent means of generating new gifts at the $500 level, and after 20 months, the endeavor generated more than $180,000. In addition, Medical Center employees have wholeheartedly supported the project. About one fourth of the funds raised have been from employees, most of whom are first-time donors.

The $500 gift could be given at one time or pledged annually over a period of three years. However, the foundation's gift policy emphasized that the Honor Roll pledge was separate and apart from other gifts.

Funds raised from the Honor Roll of Women were designated to enhance women's health care services, although donors were able to designate their gift elsewhere.

The foundation promoted the Honor Roll through newsletters, committees, and personal contacts. An attractive brochure provided information about the Honor Roll and the new Women's Hospital. At the contributor's request, the foundation also mailed a lovely card of appreciation to the honored woman, informing her of the gift made in her honor.

Vogel emphasizes that this project was enjoyable and personally rewarding, "Such meaning is going into this," she added. "It has been a pure joy to do it."

38

Use Naming Opportunities to Encourage Gifts and Recognize Donors

Naming opportunities are usually reserved for a few important donors. However, naming opportunities abound at Botsford General Hospital in Farmington Hills, Michigan, where more than 55 donors have chosen to contribute $7,500 or more and have their names inscribed on brass site plaques throughout the hospital. The naming opportunities are part of a donor recognition program developed for a five-year, $5 million campaign project.

"Our recognition program is a key aspect of good donor stewardship at the hospital," says Bonnie Wood, former director of development. The following is the five-step recognition program used at Botsford:

1.   A personalized gift acknowledgment is mailed within 24 hours to every donor, regardless of gift amount.

2.   Each donor is given a bronze, silver or gold enameled lapel pin. The color indicates the level of support. In addition, donors at the $5,000 and above level receive gifts ranging from paperweights to director emeritus status at the hospital.

3.   All campaign donors have their names inscribed on the Campaign Donor Wall.

4.   Donors of $5,000 or more have brass plaques inscribed and placed on the Allen Zieger, D.O. tribute wall.

5. Donors of $7,500 may choose a naming opportunity at the hospital. At the selected site, a brass plaque acknowledges each gift with the name of the donor or of someone to be honored or remembered.

An attractive color catalog of naming opportunities presents lists of available site plaque locations along with maps showing where these areas are located in the hospital. The locations on the map are color keyed to indicate the gift level needed to support that particular room or area. Site plaque opportunities range from $7,500 for an admitting office to $750,000 for the entire emergency department.

During the recent campaign, more than 55 people chose places for site plaques. An additional $100,000 in gifts was received from those wishing to increase or make new gifts in order to receive site plaque eligibility. (Not everyone eligible for a site plaque chose to do so.)

Development officials promoted the naming opportunities with information placed in internal newsletters. They also mailed the naming opportunities brochure to physicians, eligible donors, vendors, and businesses. "We were not overly aggressive, so donors did not feel pressured," adds Wood.

Wood says the response to the naming opportunities was "extremely positive, inspiring, and motivational," and she feels the program would work for many organizations, from hospitals to schools. The Botsford program will continue now that the successful campaign is over. In addition, they are also offering smaller donors of $100 or $200 the opportunity to have their names or the names of loved ones inscribed on bricks for a pathway in their Tribute Memorial Garden.

Educational Area		$10,000	Transcription Area
$50,000 ea.	Two Classrooms	$7,500	Cytology
		$7,500	Frozen Section Room
Laboratory		$7,500	Gross Cutting Room
$100,000	Entire General	$7,500	Slide Storage Area
	Chem/Hem Area	$7,500	Lab Director's
$35,000	Histology/Cytology		Secretary's Office
	Lab Area		
$35,000	Transfusion Services	**Microbiology**	
$25,000	Pathology Conf. Room	$10,000	Inoculation Area
$25,000	Entire Microbio. Area	$10,000 ea.	Two Lab Stations
$15,000	Computer Room		
$15,000	Phlebotomy Room	**Pathology**	
$15,000	Lab Serv. Waiting Area	$70,000	Entire Administration
$15,000	Teaching Microscope Rm.	$25,000	Director's Office
$10,000	Lab Director's Office	$10,000 ea.	Three Pathologists'
$10,000	Lounge		Offices
$10,000	Lab Reception Area	$10,000	Residents' Office
$10,000	Eight Lab Stations	$10,000	Office

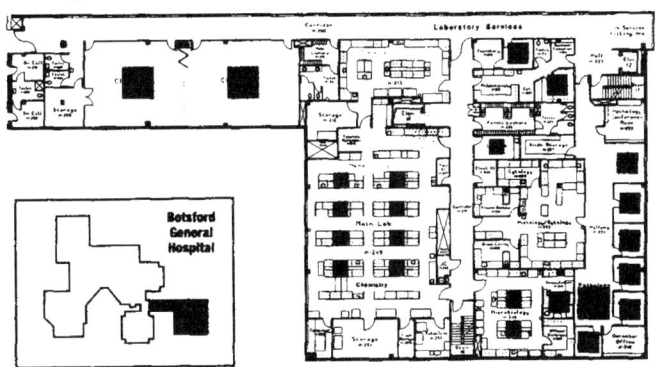

Botsford General Hospital naming opportunities were identified based on gift size.

39

Saying "Thank You" May be as Important as Soliciting the Gift

"They can buy a room."
"They can buy a building."
"We can give them this piece of crystal."
"We can have their name put on a plaque in the building."

Often, when nonprofit organizations address the need to recognize donors, the discussion degenerates into statements such as those above.

A senior member of a planning committee—a man who spent his career as the head of the trust department of a major banking interest—stood before an organization discussing donor recognition and said, "You know, I am not sure how much recognition any one of these people really wants. What we need to think about is how to say 'thank you.'"

The real issue of recognition is showing appreciation or saying "thank you." This is an issue of vital importance that often gets relegated and delegated to staff members when volunteer input is critical.

Organizations should develop not only a recognition policy, which will vary in terms of its profile, glitter, and glamour, but also a "gift appreciation" policy.

A gift appreciation policy provides guidelines on some of the formalities of saying "thank you" such as a letter of thanks being mailed within 24 hours of the receipt of a gift and letters of appreciation from members of the leadership. As an example, gifts of more than $2,500 should receive thank you letters from the president and campaign chair, etc.

But appreciation goes much further than that. Here are several examples of how others have demonstrated and expressed appreciation:

- A hospital in Canada found it effective to have members of its board call donors of $100 or more—not to ask for another gift—but just to say "thank you." The hospital also used those conversations as a means for conducting additional prospect research.

- One donor, who has given away millions of dollars, shared the most effective expression of thanks he ever received: an organization in Kansas serving disabled children took a picture of two children lying on the floor with alphabet blocks that spelled out, "Thank you, Mr. Clark."

- Institutions that manage endowment funds have a fiduciary and stewardship responsibility to indicate to their donors the status of those funds. However, many institutions do not meet that basic responsibility. Recently, a hospital in Missouri began sharing with its donors the economic status and use of endowed funds. The information was given through a hand-delivered, personal letter and detailed report relating the recent activity of the funds.

- A ballet company in Oklahoma offered its donors an inscribed ballet slipper saying, "Thank you for your gift." One donor cherishes that token as the most meaningful recognition she has received—a simple pink ballet slipper.

- The leadership of one institution privately informed the fellow alumni class members of one donor about his significant gift, and encouraged them to send personal, handwritten notes extending their appreciation of his generosity. Imagine the heartfelt gratitude of the donor and his family as these letters arrived.

- Following the receipt of a significant endowed gift, one arts organization included a photograph and biographical information about the donor in the program. The information was distributed during one of its major concert series and the organization committed to do that each year, in perpetuity.

Sometimes concern about the confidentiality of a gift keeps an organization from sharing the names of donors with board members. However, it is the board's fiduciary responsibility as owners of the organization to have that information. They are aware of other funding that comes to the agency. More importantly, the knowledge provides an opportunity for individuals, generally of the same social group, to comment informally to the donor about the importance of a gift.

Expressing thanks for a gift is always important, but acknowledging the timing of a gift if it comes when the staff is discouraged, the volunteers are exhausted, and there is no positive end in sight, is especially important. Share the particulars of why the gift is so appreciated. Help donors understand the revitalization and renewed commitment their gifts have brought to the staff and leadership.

Good stewardship is not just sending a receipt for a gift. The banker was right, an organization can do a lot of things to celebrate a gift, but the important thing is to properly say "thank you".

Special Ways to Say "Thank You"

Expressing appreciation to donors does not need to be expensive, but it should be sincere and special. Try to make donor recognition a personal and genuine experience. Here are some ideas:

- Regional books, magazines or newspapers subscriptions for donors who live far away
- A new tree planted in tribute
- A video or photo album of a project's construction or renovation (from start to finish)
- A packet of seeds accompanying a personal note, "Your gift sowed the seeds that will benefit others for generations to come."
- Personalized gift baskets
- A multi-signature signed card
- A personal message on a marquee or outdoor advertising
- A limited-edition pastel drawing of a landmark
- A mention on the home page of the organization's World Wide Web site

40

Identify Ways to Demonstrate Gratitude

It is much more cost effective to retain donors than it is to secure new ones. For that reason alone, it is worth taking the time to express gratitude to those who have made contributions throughout the year. It is also important to remember that the price of a thank you is much less important than the sincerity of appreciation.

Here are some ways to express appreciation to donors throughout the year:

- Mail thank you letters within 48 hours after receiving a gift.

- Phone or stop by immediately to express appreciation for larger gifts. Thank you visits make future solicitation visits more palatable.

- Use handwritten letters as opposed to typed letters when feasible. They need not be lengthy, but tend to make a communication much more meaningful.

- Ask those served by the organization to express appreciation— college students, patients, youth. Those who are served by the generosity of others can best say, "thank you."

- Give donors a gift that says thanks. Depending on the size of the gift and the type of nonprofit, recognition gifts can be appropriate. Select gifts that include the name of the organization or the logo— letter openers, paperweights, mugs, plaques, lapel pins. Consider meaningful gifts that are tied to the organization—art pieces made by college students, bookmarks made by youth, etc.—as a way of expressing appreciation.

- Publicly thank donors in the organization's publications. List donors in the newsletter and profile donors and gifts in feature articles and news releases.

- Host special events for the benefit of special donors. Consider a once- or twice-a-year reception for those contributing at a certain level.

- Cite examples, not statistics. Rather than telling past contributors how many people their gifts have helped, cite one or two real-life examples that will capture their attention and convey the impact of their gifts. Real life examples make the gift giving much more rewarding for donors.

41

What to do Once the Campaign is Over

Once the campaign is over, the natural instinct is to rest. Actually, this is the time to evaluate the campaign while laying the groundwork for the future.

The campaign is concluded; the goal is met. The party to celebrate the success is almost over. The mood has never been so high and at the same time, so low. Colleagues look at one another and ask, "What do we do now that the campaign is complete?"

A campaign is an intense undertaking no matter how small or large the goal. The following are some essential steps for proper closure of a campaign:

1) **Acknowledgement of donors.** It is amazing the number and size of additional gifts that result from the pleasure donors receive from being recognized for their first gift. Therefore, be sure to:

—Review the named gift opportunities. As soon as possible, meet with the persons, businesses, and foundations that qualify for such recognition and discuss the options available to them.

—Encourage the architect and contractor to work on appropriate ways to show recognition. The properties of this recognition need not be extravagant, but should be tasteful. This activity will be important to future support and giving.

161

2) **Board development.** A successful campaign is an asset in the process of identifying, strategizing, and soliciting prospective board members. Identify good prospects that have surfaced as a result of the campaign.

3) **Keep in touch during construction or program development.** During the construction phase of the campaign or the evolution of the new program, it is important to update donors continuously. At least every other week, the fund raiser and a board member should host a lunch and brief tour of the facility. These construction updates can be simple and direct, but need to relate to the focus of the organization's mission.

   At least six months prior to the due date of the final pledge payment, hold meetings with donors to discuss their feelings about the success of the campaign. Get ideas for the future and assess their interest in continuing support. Obviously, no solicitation should take place.

   Following the final gift payment, hold meetings with donors to discuss an ongoing support pledge. For example, if someone has given $25,000 in two or three payments, develop a series of projects where they might invest a minimum of $1,000 or as much as $5,000 per year.

4) **Honor staff and volunteers.** Give credit to the volunteers and staff who have made the campaign a success.

   Develop an activity associated with a board meeting or other event for recognition of the leadership and support group. Again, quality and taste should dominate this recognition.

5) **Review items not funded.** If there are specific elements of the campaign not satisfied, review any prospects that might be specifically oriented to this type of project and solicit those prospects.

6) **Annual fund.** This is the time to establish new methods of annual support. Short- and long-term plans should be developed and established for annual fund-raising with specific achievable targets.

7) **Campaign evaluation.** It is vital to prepare a simple questionnaire to be completed by the campaign leadership concerning the strengths and weaknesses of the campaign.

8) **Use the recommendations that come from the questionnaire when formulating a specific post-campaign plan.** This plan will serve as a road map to the future for the extension of development efforts, as well as the preparation of the next campaign.

9) **The next campaign.** The methods and contacts developed can and must sustain the institution and prepare it for the next special effort. The information gathered about donors, prospects, foundations, and individuals should be input and retained on your system and easily reviewed. Develop a prospect list and keep it current. Keep prospects involved in preparation for future projects.

A successful campaign leads people to expect the same level of success in the future. When volunteers, staff, and institutional leadership have set a very high standard, the next thought will be, "That was a good campaign, but what have you done for me recently?" Take every possible step to ensure the success of the organization's next effort.

Public Announcement

42

Use a Public Announcement

The public announcement for a campaign follows the quiet phase. At this time, approximately 50 percent of a campaign goal should be committed. Frequently, this percentage goes as high as 70 to 80 percent. The public announcement serves to inform those who have yet to make a contribution to the campaign.

So far, each step of the campaign has unfolded as planned: a long-term strategic plan was developed and from that, a compelling case statement was written and shared with major gift prospects and board members.

A campaign plan was developed and endorsed by the board. A steering committee was assembled and its members have quietly been securing lead gifts. According to the schedule, 50 to 80 percent or more of the campaign goal has been secured from board members and a handful of others (as few as 10 percent of the constituency), and the organization is about to go public with an official announcement of the campaign.

The public announcement of a campaign is an important phase of the overall process. It is at this point that the remaining 90 percent of the constituency are expected to respond generously with multi-year commitments.

Here are some strategies to help publicly announce the campaign:

1) **Schedule a well thought-out press conference.** Have board members, the steering committee, and major gift participants on hand for the CEO's public announcement of the campaign. Unveil plans to the media for the use of the funds. Show a scale of giving for

167

the campaign that illustrates as much as 50 to 80 percent of the goal has already been met. Distribute campaign press packets. If it can be accomplished, announce a challenge gift that has been established in which all future commitments will be matched dollar for dollar. Personalize the announcement to potential donors. Send an invitation for public announcement to area prospects. At least, send a personalized letter announcing and explaining the campaign to those slated to be approached. (Do not, however, ask for any kind of commitment at this time.)

2) **Periodically announce major gifts that were committed during the quiet phase of the campaign.** To help maintain the campaign's momentum following the announcement, schedule weekly or monthly announcements of major gifts and feature stories on how they will be earmarked for the campaign. Focus on how gifts will benefit those served by the organization.

3) **Inform prospects outside of the immediate area.** When counting on the help of individuals, businesses, or foundations from outside the immediate geographic area, take steps to include them in the public announcement of the campaign. Send a video of the campaign announcement. Schedule area receptions to restage the announcement for those in each location.

4) **Enlist solicitor volunteers who have or will make significant gifts during this most visible period.** Once the most major gift prospects have been approached during the pre-announcement phase, enlist those prospects on the next level of financial capability as volunteers in the effort. Approach them individually for a commitment to become involved as a volunteer. Volunteers will tend to contribute more sacrificially if they become involved in and "own" the campaign and, likewise, will be better volunteer solicitors if they have made exemplary commitments themselves.

Be Mindful of Donor Needs

Donors do not give major gifts because an organization needs money. They give them because of their own needs. The sooner the donor's needs are identified, the sooner the gift can be closed. This is one reason successful fund raisers spend so much time cultivating the prospective donor. Keep thinking about how a gift can benefit the donor.

43

Ground Breakings With Pizzazz

When an organization plans a new facility, it wants the highest possible level of community participation. Construction offers many opportunities to celebrate and to increase an awareness of the organization's mission. Here are some ideas and time frames for festivities and news coverage throughout the process:

- **Start with the architect's rendering.** Use the drawing to create a fund-raising brochure with an envelope for pledges. Include lots of facts about how the building will enhance services. Make full-color copies of the rendering to use with press releases about the new addition.

- **Ask supporters and employees to think of items for a "time capsule."** A ground breaking ceremony can be more fun with the burial of a time capsule full of items significant to the organization's history. Also invite those attending to sign a banner or cloth to put inside; they will enjoy their participation in a memorable event.

- **Invite a well-known local or regional celebrity to participate.** Ideally, that person will have some interest in the organization's mission and be able to make brief remarks. Present him or her with a decorated honorary shovel or hard hat as a souvenir, and take plenty of photos for later press releases or publications.

169

- **Pour a cement slab.** Then let board members, employees, and supporters leave a thumbprint, initials, a colorful stone, a utensil used in their work or other type of memento in the cement to harden. If the results are attractive and artistic, the slab can be set someplace inside or outside the new structure. Be sure soap, water, towels, and lotion are on hand for those who use bare hands.

- **Hold an outdoor picnic for all ages.** Have a large tent, refreshments, games, speeches, and even a contest for a facility name, if one has not been chosen. Offer colorful toy shovels for the children in attendance, and let them "break ground" themselves. The photo opportunities alone are priceless, and can be used in ongoing fund-raising literature.

- **Take an aerial photo of supporters encircling the area.** Ask everyone attending to form a line, holding hands if there are enough people, around the perimeter of the building's future walls. Instead of the stakes and strings or flags usually used by construction crews to mark the boundaries, use colorful ribbons and posts. Dignitaries may stand in the center to turn over the first shovels. Write a speech that promotes future, hope, and unity to be read by the speaker.

Campaign Successes

44

Gifts from the Heart
YWCA of Tulsa

The Young Women's Christian Association has been a caring neighbor in the Tulsa community since its arrival in 1914. After years of active service, the YWCA facilities were in need of substantial rebuilding and renovations. Plans for a campaign began in the early 1990s and years of fact-gathering followed. In 1993 the YWCA kicked off its first attempts with a campaign readiness program.

Around this time, a capital funds campaign goal was set for between three to five million dollars. The campaign advisory committee was established and after reviewing all available information, they concluded that there was a well-established need for new facilities. Unfortunately, the committee further realized that the YWCA was unprepared for such a huge campaign undertaking.

Four to Six Million

Four million dollars. FOUR MILLION DOLLARS! The thought was absolutely overwhelming; but so was the need. Everyone knew how important it was to meet this fund-raising goal, but could it really be done? Still apprehensive, yet driven with conviction, no one could imagine what lay ahead for the YWCA of Tulsa, Oklahoma. What had been their destination became just another short stop on the way to something that surpassed even hidden hopes. By the time they were finished, they had reached six million dollars. SIX MIL-

LION DOLLARS! Success is defined as finishing with a favorable outcome. This was beyond success. This was breathtaking!

Keep the Momentum Going

No one on the board had experience organizing or running a fund-raising campaign and records of past donors were incomplete. "It was hard continuing to sustain a belief in the campaign at that time, and it was difficult to keep up the momentum. The whole process was so new to the organization, and a campaign is layered on top of the everyday things you must do just to keep the doors open," offered Kathleen Page, who then served as president of the board of directors.

In February 1994, the campaign effort suffered another setback. Due to staffing changes, they faced an immediate need for effective leadership in both the organization and in a major fund-raising venture. For the time being, the campaign advisory committee was disbanded, and plans for a campaign were put on indefinite hold.

Although the focus of the YWCA shifted to internal operations during 1994 and much of 1995, the dream of a campaign still lingered. By April 1995, they were working on a new campaign action plan, which included a more comprehensive approach. By September of that year, a planning committee was in place. And by December, the YWCA further committed staff resources to the campaign effort by hiring Dixie Reppe as director of development and public relations, with the primary task of providing staff direction for the campaign. In February 1996, board members Pat Bailey and Mary Ann Meckfessel agreed to serve as campaign co-chairs.

Making a Commitment

With things moving into place, a real turning point came in March 1996 when board members met with a fund-raising consulting firm. In May, the YWCA retained the firm, and immediately began formulating a more full-fledged campaign plan.

After an initial study, the firm concluded that the YWCA lacked both individual and institutional fund-raising experience—after all, the organization had not staged a major campaign since 1954, and had never undertaken one of this proportion. The firm recommended how the campaign should be organized, helped set priorities, and identified additional sources of funding.

"Up to that point, we frankly didn't know how to ask for money, and we didn't know who to ask," says Meckfessel. "We had done very little in terms of going into the community, and didn't know what foundations were out there and what kinds of programs they funded. The consultant opened our eyes to all of that, and showed us how to set up a structure for the campaign."

"We had to totally learn how to do it," Bailey added. "In the beginning we approached people who we had some history with personally. But the consultant gave us the confidence and know-how to approach others."

In addition to coaching Bailey and others during regular campaign meetings, the consultant debriefed team members after campaign calls and offered valuable feedback to hone their fund-raising skills. As the campaign gained impetus, the consultant also helped the team develop increasingly effective strategies to reach and connect prospective donors with the important work being done by the YWCA.

"The consultant always stressed the importance of respecting the donor—seeing things through their eyes, through their concerns and interests and converting that into something that was mutually beneficial," shared Reppe. "He helped to build a team that functioned well together. Every meeting with the consultant was like a class in fund raising. He asked questions and then gave us direction and instruction that increased our confidence and improved our fund-raising abilities."

Although the firm had initially advised a goal of $4 million—due to the organization's lack of fund-raising history—campaign leaders felt that a larger amount was necessary to fully meet the needs of the YWCA. With a growing confidence from the campaign team as their efforts proved more and more successful, the goal was increased over time, first to $4.4 million, then to $5 million, and ultimately to $6 million.

Major Gifts Give Confidence

The YWCA received several significant commitments, including major pledges from companies and foundations. Some of their requests were successful beyond their wildest dreams. In October 1997, for example, the campaign received a major boost with an $850,000 challenge grant from The J.E. & L.E. Mabee Foundation of Tulsa. In addition, in March 1998 the YWCA was notified that The Kresge Foundation was issuing a challenge grant of $500,000. This achievement was all the more impressive because The Kresge Foundation, based in Troy, Michigan, receives up to 9,000 requests a year from organizations across the nation—and awards only about 100 grants.

Gifts great and small were received with sincere appreciation and the YWCA experienced an outpouring of support from individuals, businesses, and foundations throughout the community. The campaign leadership was particularly proud of the fact that 100 percent of the board of directors and staff were contributors to the campaign. A $1 million endowment from Pat and Keith Bailey served to further the level of enthusiasm and commitment for the campaign.

Another special gift is remembered by Dixie Reppe, "A woman who suffered with arthritis received some relief from the use of our aquatic facilities. Although she had limited assets, she wanted to show her appreciation and respect for the help that the YWCA offered others. She owned a piece of property just outside of Tulsa that she deeded over to the YWCA, which translated into a gift of $10,000. Greater than the amount of the gift, was the act of generosity and show of support that it represented."

The Final Gift

On October 1, 1998, the YWCA accepted the gift that "put them over the top." A $125,000 check from Edward L. Gaylord completed their ambitious campaign goal and sealed their success. This poignant gift was made in honor of his mother, Inez Kinney Gaylord, who had served as the first executive secretary of the YWCA West Central Field Committee and played an important role in its beginning back in 1913. Now, a generation later, her son was playing an important role in its future.

"This campaign was run by people who have a heart for the YWCA," Reppe said. Clearly, a campaign of this magnitude took a lot of time and effort. "We learned to maximize our abilities and use them in various combinations as, in groups of two or three, we took our case to the generous people of Tulsa. Donors want to know everything about the organization—who you are, what your mission is, and how you help people. That's the story we never grew weary of telling. The tangible response we experienced suggests our message was heard."

45

Meeting a Critical Need

Epworth Villa

Epworth Villa, a not-for-profit life care retirement community in Oklahoma City, addressed a critical need for high quality dementia care with a vision for what this care should be, followed by a carefully developed plan. This combination produced a campaign that was successful beyond the agency's most ambitious plans.

Founded in 1990, Epworth Villa had almost no fund raising track record. It had a donor base of 186 donors, with only one gift of $25,000 and no foundation grants. Previous annual campaigns raised between $30,000 to $40,000 and there were no outside volunteers.

Yet, Epworth Villa raised $6.5 million in less than two years. This included gifts from 564 donors ranging from five dollars to $1 million, seven foundation gifts totaling almost $2 million and a volunteer structure that involved 70 volunteers.

How was this possible? Need combined with vision and careful planning created a formula for success.

Dementia Care Needed

A critical need for dementia care existed in Oklahoma City. When the project was first conceived there were less than 500 beds dedicated to dementia care. Yet, there were over 20,000 people living with dementia in the area.

Epworth Villa staff and board judiciously studied this problem of dementia care. Former CEO/president Joe White visited 30 successful programs throughout the country. Using information from these visits, he and the staff worked with a consultant to form a concept and architectural drawings.

The project that developed was both visionary and practical. It included a 48-bed dementia center, a 20-person adult day care center, and a community outreach program. The dementia center will be environmentally therapeutic while retaining homelike features. The community outreach component includes caregiver training and support and a research agreement with the University of Oklahoma College of Nursing and Oklahoma City University School of Nursing. The new care techniques developed through the university relationships will be disseminated directly to caregivers through the Epworth Villa community outreach.

Assessment of Potential

A market study and financial campaign assessment were conducted to determine if there was a market for dementia care and if Epworth Villa could financially support such an ambitious project. Once these results were in, the Epworth Villa board gave the project a go-ahead.

Getting Started

Initial foundation contacts were made. As a result of these, The Samuel Roberts Noble Foundation issued a challenge grant. This challenge not only served as the lead gift, but also gave the campaign legitimacy with the Epworth Villa residents, the board and the Oklahoma City community.

Armed with this challenge and a deadline, Epworth Villa issued a request for proposals to eight fund-raising consulting firms. Three were invited to Oklahoma City for interviews before one was selected.

The campaign consultant's first act was to conduct a campaign assessment study. The campaign assessment study demonstrated support for the project, set the goal at $6 million (which was later revised to $6.5 million) and developed a viable campaign strategy.

One aspect of the consultant's strategy that proved to be most successful was the aggressive solicitation of bequests and planned gifts. In a retirement community where the average age is over 80, estate gifts can count their full value. The Epworth Villa campaign raised over $2 million in estate gifts.

178

Establishing Leadership

After the board reviewed the study and plan of action, volunteer leadership was recruited. G.T. Blankenship, former Oklahoma Attorney General and current University of Oklahoma Regent, immediately recognized the need for the project and willingly agreed to serve as campaign chair.

A story to demonstrate the impact of Blankenship's dedication to the project occurred about halfway through the campaign. Epworth Villa senior staff and Blankenship had a Monday morning appointment with the trustees of the Mabee Foundation in Tulsa, Oklahoma, about two hours away from Oklahoma City. The day before Blankenship and the other university regents had spent most of the day in a highly publicized firing of the OU football coach. The Mabee Foundation trustees who were OU football fans were most impressed when Blankenship showed up for the appointment. This display of Blankenship's dedication to the project helped garner a Mabee Foundation grant.

Many other volunteers were also inspired by the vision of the project. Luke Luker, an Epworth Villa resident, provided much needed resident leadership by serving as campaign vice chair. His belief in the project and his willingness to make a significant gift quieted resident skepticism and enabled him to recruit a working team.

Ausin Troxel, an Epworth Villa resident, was willing to serve as the major gifts chair because he wanted to build a better place for his wife who was living with Alzheimer's disease. Troxel was so enthusiastic about his fund raising that he often joked no one would eat lunch with him any more. The campaign was about five months old when Troxel's wife suddenly died of pneumonia. Troxel, though, continued to be inspired by the vision of what quality care could do for those living with Alzheimer's. As a result of this, Troxel helped raise $1 million.

The Initial Challenge

It took less than two months to get the campaign committees staffed and meeting regularly. Then the consultant challenged the campaign leadership to make the Mabee Foundation December deadline. In order to do this volunteers and staff would need to raise over $3 million in six months. This was a big challenge for an organization that had never raised $1 million.

Board and volunteers were doubtful that this challenge could be met. The consultant continued to encourage and provide counsel and strategies for ways to meet his challenge. In spite of this, the campaign struggled.

Then, when things were looking the darkest and spirits were the lowest, a resident's family stepped forward with a million-dollar gift. The family had

179

been discussing a gift with Franci Hart, Epworth Villa's development officer, for some time. However, they had not indicated the magnitude of the gift until they made the announcement.

This gift proved to be the turning point of the campaign. Once this gift was announced the campaign volunteers and board realized that it would be possible to raise the rest of the money needed to meet the Mabee Foundation's criteria. The Mabee Foundation stipulates that half of a campaign goal must be raised before approaching the trustees. Three and one half million dollars were raised. The Mabee Foundation issued a challenge grant. This challenge grant led to positive responses from other foundations.

The Vision and Need

The need for dementia care, Epworth Villa's vision to meet this need and the consultant's carefully developed campaign plan of action were the winning plays to this campaign. On December 21, 1999, less than two years after the campaign committees began meeting, the Epworth Villa campaign celebrated its successful conclusion with a surprise party for the Epworth Villa residents. The campaign total at that time was $6,636,000.

46

Building Tomorrow ... Girl by Girl
Girl Scout Council of the Ozark Area

G irl Scouting has a long history in the Ozark area, going back at least to 1922. As Girl Scout councils continued to expand and combine, new councils emerged. The Girl Scout Council of the Ozark Area (GSCOA), starting under its current jurisdiction in 1956, is one of 318 councils chartered by Girl Scouts of the USA. The Council is charged with administering the Girl Scout program in ten counties: five in southwest Missouri (Vernon, Barton, Jasper, Newton, and McDonald), three in southeast Kansas (Bourbon, Crawford, and Cherokee), and two in northeast Oklahoma (Ottawa and Delaware).

Before Building Tomorrow ... Girl by Girl, GSCOA had never attempted a capital campaign. Fund raising was still an uncomfortable subject for many board members before 1990. Major universities were just entering the fund raising arena in a big way and bringing with them a new image of asking. For some board members in the Midwest and especially in Joplin, Missouri, the idea of going to the community for money had negative implications—fund raising was still considered a euphemism for begging. By early 1994, that view had changed. The Council was working hard to enhance visibility and increase its efforts among girls not typically served by Girl Scouts.

Serving the Underserved

A new emphasis on underserved populations of girls led GSCOA to address contemporary issues such as teen pregnancy and school drop-out rates.

Outreach programs and services were started for girls with special needs and circumstances i.e., an Oklahoma Native American reserve troop, Hispanic mission troops, and specialized programs to deal with the rising incidence of teen pregnancy.

The Guardian Angel Program (GAP) was developed to provide unique, self-esteem building projects for girls who, due to socio-economic circumstances, would not otherwise have access to the advantages of participating in Girl Scouts. GAP programs offered throughout the Joplin, Miami and Webb City areas include:

- **Breakfast Clubs**—Presented by Council staff and volunteers during the school day in lower income area schools.

- **Boys & Girls Club Troops**—Programs at the Boys & Girls Club including Brownie Girl Scouts (grades 1 - 3), Junior Girl Scouts (grades 3 - 6), and Cadette Girl Scouts (grades 6 - 9).

- **Summer Programs at the Boys & Girls Club**—Designed to involve at-risk youth in fun, hands-on activities.

- **Daisy Head Start Program**—Targeting pre-kindergarten aged girls and their mothers in 25 head start schools located throughout the council's 10-county jurisdiction.

- **Ozark Center Intensive Treatment Unit Lock Down Unit**—Delivering weekly programs to girls who have been institutionalized.

- **Ozark Center Group Home (Turn Around Ranch)**—An effort to reach underserved girl populations.

GSCOA made extraordinary efforts to serve areas that remained unreached: rural and poorer areas, non-traditional settings such as institutions, and girls that were without transportation or strong parental support.

The capital campaign was necessary not only for new programming, but for improvements to Ozark Girl Scout camp's 50-year aging infrastructures and facilities. A portion of the campaign goal was earmarked for a new activity lodge, a camp challenge course with rappelling tower as well as an Education and Service Center for Girls. In addition to administrative offices, the new Center includes a computer lab complete with the latest technology and internet access.

Optimism and Commitment

The 1997 campaign assessment suggested a total price tag of $2.2 million, with $500,000 designated toward a maintenance endowment. The results, announced in January 1997, preceded Board approval in March of the same year.

"I really went into the campaign with lots of optimism and very little fund raising experience," said Karen Morgan, executive director for GSCOA since 1990. "I simply thought, 'If other organizations have done it, why can't we?' I never doubted that we would be successful. However, I never dreamed it would be so difficult."

The campaign had the unusual challenge of engaging three different development directors over the course of the campaign. Nothing tabloid-worthy, just bad timing for GSCOA. Despite this anomaly, the campaign kept moving.

"One thing I learned is that success is not how quickly you finish the campaign," offered Morgan. "Success is sticking with it and finishing the campaign goal. I received e-mails from other executive directors. They were not always encouraging. Some told of their lack of success and gave discouraging reports from their own campaigns."

Another challenge for the agency was to develop a steering committee with members who knew about the Girl Scout program and were personal advocates. For the most part, initial steering committee members were not affiliated with Girl Scouts. They did not come in with a history of involvement with the organization. Relationships needed to be developed with individuals who already had an interest and a passion for the mission, and who were not already financially committed elsewhere. This took some work.

Building Momentum

An official campaign announcement came in 1998 after some momentum building. The board president made a lead gift, followed by the steering committee chair and others. One hundred percent board and steering committee financial participation established the campaign further. Gifts started arriving and in addition, the Council received a gift of land worth $216,000 at fair market value.

In the spring of 2000, a local foundation opened its doors for the first time to agencies that received United Way gifts. This was great timing for the Building Tomorrow campaign, since United Way has been a strong financial supporter of the Girl Scouts. The foundation's donation of $150,000 turned out later to be the key to receiving a J.E. and L.E. Mabee Foundation grant of $200,000. A gift of $150,000 came from a local foundation in Carthage, Missouri and a $25,000 gift from the C. W. Titus Foundation. There was also a

Kemper Foundation gift of $15,000 and another local foundation added $150,000 to the campaign. A utility company donated $25,000 and a bank gave $25,000. Other local corporations jumped in with gifts of various amounts and several individuals made $10,000 donations. The Lemons Trust donated another $100,000 to the campaign.

Not only did the capital campaign help to overcome old fund-raising perceptions, but the heightened visibility actually brought greater prestige and new donor friends for GSCOA. "I really learned the significance of the old adage: It is not what you know, it is who you know," added Morgan. "People handed me checks and said that the gift was given because they knew me and knew about the changes we were making in programming and outreach."

As is often the case, the annual fund took a hit while the campaign was in full swing. At the consultant's recommendation, the organization hired a second person to assist with annual giving and to help with communications during the campaign. Anticipating this additional need, and addressing it before it became a crisis, helped in practical ways. It also helped sustain morale and energy while the agency juggled two important fund raising ventures.

"This campaign would not have occurred without the vision of the executive director, Karen Morgan. She receives much credit for this campaign," said the campaign counsel." As with all successful campaigns, there were excellent leaders among the staff, including Tiffany Brooks, the development director for much of the campaign and its finished goal, and superior volunteers epitomized by Rita Bicknell and Frances Nichols."

"Our consultant helped keep us on track," offered former Girl Scout development director, Tiffany Brooks. "He was always there to reassure us and point us in the right direction. He prompted us to start a monthly newsletter. The First Monday Memo was helpful in keeping donors aware of our progress. One thing I personally learned from the campaign was the importance of keeping in touch with potential donors. Gifts that we thought were impossible came through after months of sending updates and personal notes. Also, personal participation in local civic groups and organizations helped to give the organization and the campaign added visibility. Potential donors who may not accept a solicitation from an organization, may accept one from a member of a mutual civic group."

Harder Than Expected, but Worth It

"The campaign was much harder than I expected," said Morgan, "but we experienced some wonderful successes along the way. We were pleased to obtain $250,000 in state tax credits. Other agencies had received tax credits in prior years, but we were the only agency in Joplin to get the state tax credits that year. It was also the first year that the Neighborhood Assistance Program required outcome measures."

The new Education and Service Center was designated to receive the financial benefit from these credits. The minimum contribution allowed was $2,500. A gift of $10,000, for example, could be deducted from federal tax as a charitable contribution. After that, 50 percent—in this case, $5,000—could be used against state taxes owed. If a donor had more credits than taxes owed, the credits could be carried over for an additional five years. Receiving Neighborhood Assistance Program tax credits allowed GSCOA to gain donors from many more community businesses and individuals than it might have otherwise.

The dedication ceremony for the Education and Service Center for Girls was held June 28, 2000. National Executive Director of The Girl Scouts of the USA, Marsha Johnson Evans, was on hand to speak and to share in the excitement. Evans congratulated and complimented GSCOA, "You are a pacesetter Council for the nation." Evans was speaking primarily about the ground breaking work the Council had achieved in providing Girl Scout opportunities for disadvantaged girls, the impressive new Education and Service Center, and the continued efforts to provide role models and leadership opportunities for another generation of girls.

However, the same thing can be said of the Girl Scout Council of the Ozark Area in regard to its fund-raising efforts. Some said it would not happen ... could not happen. It took a long time, but with the $2,200,000 goal achieved, the Girl Scout Council of the Ozark Area also serves as a fund-raising pacesetter for other nonprofit organizations.

47

Campaign Destiny—To Become the Best
Iowa State University

Before the ground is turned up, before the seed is even sown, the soil plays a fundamental role in the harvest. Quality and consistency, to a large degree, determine the potential for growth. Iowa State's campaign that returned in excess of $458 million in five years, was by anyone's standards, a bumper crop. But below the surface of this well-run campaign, marked by good promotion and obvious hard work, was a belief grounded in the soil of the University. Not a hope planned by committee, but a true sense of destiny.

From ISU's own self-description, Iowa State has aspired to become the best land-grant university in the nation. This goal is very ambitious but worthy of the land-grant institution serving the state that prides itself on being number one in education. Campaign Destiny: To Become the Best was the largest fundraising initiative in Iowa State University's history.

Campaign: An Individual Success

"The efforts of many individuals made Campaign Destiny an absolutely extraordinary success, and the biggest beneficiaries of this success are ISU's students," remarked ISU President Martin Jischke. "The millions raised for scholarships increase the opportunities for students to pursue college degrees, while money for new buildings, programs, and professorships greatly enhances the quality of undergraduate and graduate education at Iowa State." Not only has the campaign opened doors, ISU has managed to open some eyes in the process.

An anonymous gift of $80 million received in 1999 was not only the largest gift to any Iowa public institution, but also the largest to any college of agriculture in the United States. Four of the top largest gifts given to any institution of higher education in the state of Iowa were given as part of Campaign Destiny. In fact, of the top 10 gifts ever received by ISU, eight came in during "...the best campaign at Iowa State."

Announced publicly in September 1996, the campaign was only halfway through its five-year counting period when contributions exceeded $224 million—three-fourths of the $300 million goal. By March 1998, the campaign hit $244 million. Later in the year, the goal was adjusted to $425 million and still surpassed.

This was Vice President of External Affairs, Murray Blackwelder's, second ISU campaign. "I arrived at Iowa State in 1991 during the Partnership for Prominence campaign. The campaign goal was to raise $100 million. It had paused around $90 million, but we got things moving and completed the campaign in 1993 with $214 million. Sometime after that campaign we uncovered a deferred gift of $34 million. The donors asked to remain anonymous and their gift represented an obvious and substantial lead gift for a new campaign."

Ultimate Gift

The husband was a graduate of ISU. The couple, living close to Iowa State's campus in Ames, had been involved in the life of the University for decades. There was a natural cultivation process occurring over that time. The husband and wife were in their nineties and both passed away prior to the end of the campaign. By 2000, the deferred gift of $34 million had matured to around $80 million. For this couple and for Iowa State, it was truly the ultimate gift.

Campaign Destiny targeted five major ISU areas: endowments, programs, buildings, financial aid, and general projects. ISU Foundation's assets burgeoned from $140 million in 1995 to $500 million in 2000. In five years the endowment grew from $84 million in 1995 to $350 million in 2000.

These gifts allowed the University to develop new curricula for undergraduate and graduate programs through initiatives such as the Center for Entrepreneurship, the Plant Sciences Institute, and ISU's first named school, the Greenlee School of Journalism and Communication. Additionally, outright and deferred gifts funded 22 new faculty professorships and chairs.

New and Renovated Construction

Over 50 building projects were advanced from the campaign. "The campaign has financed building projects throughout the campus, from the development of Reiman Gardens to the enhancement and expansion of Jack Trice Stadium," said Thomas Mitchell, ISU Foundation President.

Gifts have helped construct the Engineering Teaching and Research complex for the College of Engineering, the Palmer Human Development and Family Studies Building for the College of Family and Consumer Sciences, Kocimski Auditorium for the College of Design, the Gerdin Business Building, the Honors Building, the 4-H Extension Youth Building, and the Carver Co-Laboratory for the Plant Sciences Institute.

Campaign Destiny opened up opportunities for students in Iowa and throughout the nation with financial aid to students through scholarships, fellowships, internships, and cooperative experiences. The Greenlee School of Journalism and Communication more than tripled the money awarded prior to the campaign. Annual scholarships multiplied from $30,000 to $100,000. Donor gifts created 614 new undergraduate and graduate scholarships, including the Hixson Opportunity Awards and Presidential Scholarships for National Merit and Achievement students.

Team of Volunteers

"We had a good team," affirmed Blackwelder. "The head of the foundation, the president, and I were all major gift fund raisers. But what really made a difference was when the faculty and staff became active in the campaign. The nine deans of the various colleges were very involved in the process. We started with a strong lead gift, which provided some campaign confidence, and the rest came together very well."

"We knew after the Partnership for Prominence campaign that we had a greater base for donor support. In 1986 we had just over 20,000 donors and $10 million in outright gifts and pledges. By 1991 we had almost 40,000 donors and over $30 million in outright gifts and pledges. With the anonymous gift in 1993, it was clear ISU had the potential for another campaign."

Five-Year Campaign

The five years of campaigning positively affected ISU's capacity to receive gifts. Each year of the campaign saw new records set for the number of donors. By the fiscal year of 2000, donor involvement was at 54,083 and counting.

"Campaign Destiny was such an overwhelming success because the right ingredients came together at the right moment: a vision and a strategic plan to achieve it, involving campus partners, a strong national economy, and committed alumni and friends," added Mitchell. Fund-raising totals such as these have moved Iowa State into the top quartile in the Big 12 development rankings, up from eighth only two years ago. More importantly, Campaign Destiny's success means more resources are helping Iowa State advance its aspiration to become the best land-grant institution in the nation.

Land-grant colleges were proposed in the mid-1800s to respond to the nation's rapid industrialization and commercialization. The emergence of education for the middle class changed the face of the work force. With technology forging another new day in the way the country works, ISU is not shy about what part the University will play. "For the century ahead," declares an Iowa State brochure, "ISU unequivocally confirms that place, initiating new processes and attitudes of flexibility, adaptability, and innovation. As a knowledge-based economy restructures the workplace, the University is gathering the momentum necessary to realize its destiny while holding true to its original land-grant heritage."

As an organization destined and committed to becoming the best, Iowa State University's soil was prepared and ready for unprecedented growth. Campaign Destiny was good agronomy in action.

48

A Visitor and Education Center
Dyck Arboretum of the Plains

As naturally as prairie grass and wildflowers grow and dance along an open, wind-blown highway, the Dyck Arboretum of the Plains grew as an expression of love for the Kansas Plains and the small, rural community of Hesston. Harold and Elva Mae Dyck first began the Arboretum in the 1980s by donating the property—which was once a wheat field—and by establishing a million dollar endowment to provide for the continued care of the acreage.

Not Just Letting The Grass Grow

Harold Dyck, former director of sales with Hesston Corporation, a farm implement manufacturing operation (now named Hay and Forage), and his wife, Elva Mae, linked the work of the Arboretum to Hesston College's educational mission. The Arboretum's mission, operating under the auspices of Hesston College, was to foster an appreciation of the natural beauty of Kansas. Over a decade later, this mission remains unchanged. Successfully achieved, a natural continuation of growth occurred as thousands of visitors experienced not only the aesthetic quality of the Arboretum, but the educational opportunity that it provided.

In 1996, the Arboretum hosted over 10,000 visitors including more than 2,200 students and adults attending educational programs and events focusing on plant physiology and reproduction, plant adaptations, horticulture, the significance of Kansas natural heritage, and the preservation of habitat for wildlife. Numerous seminars on utilizing native plants in the landscape were given by staff to hundreds of people across the state including the Kansas Chapter of the Nature Conservancy, the Kansas Association of Nurserymen, the North American Prairie Conference, the Kansas State Historical Society, and the Wichita Lawn, Flower and Garden Show.

It was soon clear that such a level of activity warranted a facility adequate to sustain the growing influence of the Arboretum and its staff. In early 1996, after an intense phase of research and planning for the needs of students and visitors at the Arboretum, the Trustees authorized the development of a plan for a Visitor and Education Center on the grounds. This 3,700-square foot facility would provide a place to conduct educational programming and accommodate its many visitors.

In July 1996, a consulting firm was asked to study the feasibility of raising the funds needed to underwrite the project. Within the same month, the Arboretum received its first Kansas Community Service Tax Credit Grant for $100,000, allowing the nonprofit to offer 70 percent state income tax credit to area businesses and individuals while raising $142,850 for the work undertaken. The original goal set in 1996 was to raise $685,000 to complete the facility. With that target in mind, the work began.

"One of the smartest things we did was to realize we needed help," offered the director of the Arboretum and major fund raiser for the project, Larry Vickerman. "This was our first major fund-raising project and we knew enough to find someone who could guide us through the process. The consultant was instrumental in raising the level of professionalism and adding an element of excellence to our work."

Moving Forward and Achieving

Working in unison with Hesston College's fund-raising project, Enhancing Excellence, the Arboretum quickly began making use of the Kansas Community Service Tax Credit Grant. Remarkably, by December 1997 the entire $100,000 tax credit had been dispensed, not only from the supportive Hesston community but from surrounding areas such as Newton, Hutchinson, and Wichita, as well as others. "The consultant convinced us early on that while we had extensive backing from the town of Hesston, its leaders and its populace, practically, we needed to look at a wider giving area. Hesston was also supporting other ventures and we agreed that many Kansas communities would be interested in seeing this project succeed," said Vickerman.

Concurrent with the extending of tax credits to interested donors, grants were written and sent to several foundations around the country. "We would write the grant and send it over to the consultant to review. He helped us throughout the grant writing process," said Vickerman. By December 1996, just months into the campaign, the Arboretum received its first outright grant given by the Stanley Smith Horticultural Trust out of Berkeley, California. "That first grant was for $13,320," Vickerman quoted from memory, with the personal interest that is representative of what was successful about this campaign. "In August of '97 we received $5,000 from the Wichita-Greyhound Charities, Inc. Foundation. In September of that year we were given a cash contribution as well as an in-kind gift of services—water, sewer, gas, for example—from the town of Hesston, authorized by the City Council. The next year we received $2,500 from the Western Resources Foundation and then $7,500 a few months later from the James S. and John L. Knight Foundation. That's when things really started to get exciting."

Discipline To Make The Calls

Vickerman said that one reason he believes individuals, businesses, and foundations were so willing to get behind the project was because they could see things were moving along at a steady, even accelerating clip. "One of the most valuable things the consultant did for us was to keep us on schedule. He'd meet with us every six weeks and let us know what was needed next. We were clear on the fact that he expected it to be done, which was a good motivator. You knew you were going to have to answer to the consultant every six weeks. That certainly helped to keep us moving forward."

In July 1998 the Arboretum received a real turning-point gift from the Mabee Foundation. The grant, written in conjunction with Hesston College, allotted over $100,000 toward the Arboretum project. In that same month, they also received a second $100,000 Kansas Community Service Tax Credit Grant; and within six months this second tax credit was also dispensed, increasing their funding by another $142,850.

By the fall of 1998, the steering committee received an additional $7,000 from the Wichita-Greyhound Charities, Inc. Foundation and stood somewhere within $50,000 of the original target. Vickerman remembers, "We'd written a grant back in February 1998 to the Lied Foundation Trust asking for $50,000. At the time, we felt as though it might be a bit of a long shot, but now we were just that far away from our goal. In early December I made a call to check up on the grant. They had shown some interest over the summer so the call let them know that their gift would put us over the top." After a week of calls back and forth, answering questions from the foundation and continuing their communication, the Lied Foundation agreed to accept the grant and donate the entire $50,000 to the Arboretum project. "It was a great way to finish off the year," Vickerman added with satisfaction.

"The consultant told us it should take about two years to meet our original target amount. This turned out to be right." Now a new goal has been added—$50,000 to be earmarked for furniture and equipment. With 3,200 students and 14,000 visitors passing through the Arboretum in 1998, it is expected that the Visitor and Education Center will enjoy much use in the years to come.

49

Standing Strong
Truman Medical Center

"The quality of mercy is not strained,
It droppeth as the gentle rain from heaven
Upon the place beneath. It is twice blessed;
It blesseth him that gives and him that takes."

From Shakespeare's *Merchant of Venice*, this verse welcomes and reminds patients and visitors that while medicine and market trends may change, the mission of Truman Medical Center is literally carved in stone. This modern regional referral center has a long tradition of caring for patients regardless of their ability to pay.

From a small frame building, which was two blocks outside the city limits at its 1870 inception, to a major medical complex, the Truman Health System tangibly expresses Kansas City's commitment to provide healthcare to all its citizens.

City's Hospital Seeks Support

Truman Medical Center on Hospital Hill descends from the city's first public health facility—General Hospital. The corporation acquired its counterpart, Truman Medical Center East, in 1973. With over 100 years of growth, Truman Medical Center on Hospital Hill and Truman East have complementary missions of care and education. Both hospitals provide patients with medical

195

attention while serving as teaching hospitals for the University of Missouri-Kansas City School of Medicine.

As the largest health-care provider for the medically indigent population of Kansas City and Jackson County, Missouri, Truman Medical Center admitted 21,500 patients and handled over 400,000 visits last year. Of those, 73,000 were emergency room patients. This ratio represents a current trend in the medical community. Fifteen years ago, roughly two-thirds of hospital patients were admitted. Today, a majority receive outpatient care. A significant increase in the need for emergency room facilities and staff created logistical obstacles for many hospitals. Trends in medicine also precipitated a challenge for Truman Medical Center. Its fund-raising campaign objectives were threefold: capital and equipment; endowment for medical education; and patient care programs. Together, they totaled $20 million in need.

Specifically, Truman Medical Center recognized a pressing need for growth in the areas of acute and outpatient care. Clinics for specialized care including sickle cell, diabetes, cardiology, HIV, oral and maxillofacial surgery, neurology, oncology, podiatry, urology, and orthopedics, were becoming a necessity rather than a luxury. In addition, market-driven improvements to labor and delivery required changes to meet the increased expectations of maternity patients. As a hospital with a dual mission to serve the underserved and support medical education, Truman Medical Center was faced with a bold, clarion call to bring these needs to the attention of Kansas City's philanthropic community.

Setting the Goal

"We had a little concern about the capacity of giving available in this community to support a $20 million campaign. Truman had never undertaken a fund-raising venture in this fashion before. However, once we settled on that campaign figure, I did not doubt that we would achieve our goal," said Ned Holland, Truman board member for 26 years and current president of the Truman Medical Center Charitable Foundation.

Truman's foundation executive director, Mark Litzler, explained, "The hospital had fostered years of goodwill. Investments of care and concern in the lives of the underserved resulted in some valuable returns. Truman Medical Center had accumulated a strong portfolio of credibility and good standing in the community. This campaign was really the first time we had asked for money in a big way. As a consequence, the community responded in a big way."

Truman Medical Center started the campaign process by asking a fund-raising firm to provide a campaign assessment. "What the consultant does is ignite people to think bigger than they thought they could. He has the ability to energize board members and staff. They are persuaded and encouraged to accomplish more—and they do," offered Litzler. "One campaign goal was to develop the idea of philanthropy as a viable way to accomplish our financial goals. Our board and doctors had never thought in those terms before. This campaign changed that dramatically. The whole expectation and philosophy of philanthropy as a fiscal opportunity was new, and the results have been of great benefit."

Truman's $20 million campaign included three major components: renovations and equipment for both hospitals ($7.2 million for intensive care additions with 42-bed facilities and critical care surgery, and labor and delivery wings); programmatic patient care ($4 million); and endowment ($8.8 million, including chaired positions to attract physicians of national stature). With these goals in mind, the campaign assessment was completed in the fall of 1997 and the campaign began in early 1998.

Fourteen Gifts Provided Campaign Leadership

The campaign's objectives were supported by 14 gifts of $500,000 or more. The following highlights the major gifts received by Truman: $2 million, Peggy Sue Neal Estate; $1.5 million, Hall Family Foundation; $1.4 million, Dr. Paul and Marilee Williams; $1.1 million, Schutte Foundation and Sosland Foundation; $1 million, Miller Foundation; $800,000 each from both the Mabee Foundation and The Kresge Foundation; $500,000, H & R Block Foundation, Speas Foundation, Dr. Harry and Kay Wall, Harry and Sharon Kuba, and an anonymous board member. The Bi-Annual Truman Gala—a black-tie dinner in May 2000—marked the official completion of Truman's successful campaign. Through the efforts of the campaign, the following endowed chairs were established: The Schutte Chair in Women's Health; The Sosland Chair in Trauma Services; and The Williams Chair in Community and Family Medicine.

Success was made more impressive in the diversity of giving. Often in a campaign of this magnitude, a large percentage of money comes from a relatively small group of foundations, corporations, and individuals. Truman's campaign was truly community supported. There were 37 gifts of over $100,000 and only 14 gifts were a half million or more, with a top gift of $2 million. This campaign benefited from significant giving in the middle tier. Campaigns tend to reflect a pyramid of philanthropy. This campaign created a circle of giving.

"It was steady work for everyone over the two-year period," said Litzler. "Of course Ned Holland was there from the beginning. Don Alexander, chairman of the corporate and foundations gift committee, was tireless in his pursuit. He was able to open a lot of doors for the hospital. Four or five of our top gifts were among the biggest these foundations had ever given. We had some unusual public relations issues going on at the same time, but the consultant helped us navigate and stay on track. The hospital is in better shape today because of the campaign—and not just financially. We had four CEOs in three years. Even

197

with this 'inoperable' condition we succeeded in reaching the $20 million mark. Conventional wisdom is that the CEO will help close some significant gifts. Our strength was a clear mission that the community could understand, believe in and support."

Conclusion

Although the facilities have changed over the corporation's history, its philosophy and mission have not. Truman Medical Center's campaign was one more positive step toward providing the best medical care and education possible, despite the cost.

Said Holland, "When we started, we didn't even know what we didn't know about fund raising. We learned a great deal over the last three years. The $20 million is great for Truman Medical Center, but better still is the increased profile and philanthropic capacity we now have in the community."

50

A Culinary and Cultural Center
Guadalupe Center, Inc.

Guadalupe Center, Inc. (GCI) has a history of launching out into uncharted territory and leading the way for others. With almost 80 years of service to the Latino community of Kansas City, Missouri, GCI considered its first campaign—expanding the Guadalupe Center at 1015 Avenida Cesar E. Chavez—necessary in order to address the changing needs and interests of GCI clients.

The Center began with a similar mission in 1919. The Mexican Revolution in the early 1900s prompted an exodus of Mexican nationals from their homeland in hope of a better life north. Many stopped in the southwest states to rebuild their lives and set a new course for the future of their children. Others pressed north into Missouri and settled in the Westside community of Kansas City, Missouri.

This new land offered great opportunity, but with it, new hardships. Some schools were closed to the Mexican immigrants, parents were prohibited from shopping at certain stores, medical services were unavailable to them— opportunity was outweighed by discrimination.

Named after the patron saint of Mexico and founded as a volunteer school and clinic for Mexican immigrants, the Guadalupe Center became one of the nation's first social service agencies for Latinos. GCI began by serving Westside Mexican immigrants with the basics—education and medical attention. Since that time the Center has expanded its borders to include metropolitan Kansas City and a community of around 100,000 Latinos. In addition, GCI

199

now dispenses a greater scope of services including a bilingual preschool, a charter high school, the first and only bilingual substance abuse outpatient program in the Greater Kansas City area, a teen pregnancy prevention program, services designed for the elderly, and many other social and cultural programs and events.

The Center is a nonsectarian organization with two major affiliations: the Heart of America United Way, since 1924; and the National Council of La Raza (NCLR), since 1985. From a settlement house for Mexican immigrants to a multi-service Latino-based agency serving the metropolitan Hispanic community, GCI grew with its constituency. By the end of the 1990s, GCI was ready again to chart new territory.

The nineties saw the Latino population in Kansas City grow at a faster rate than any other ethnic group. In response to this developing resource of cultural and economic influence, GCI anticipated a need to expand its building and its programming. Expansion would not only give administrative offices breathing room, but also add a full service catering and culinary arts training program and an enhanced Latino cultural arts facility. These services were already provided by GCI, but success came with its own challenges. GCI staff could see greater opportunity just ahead, but to get there they would need to venture into the new realm of million dollar campaigns—the undiscovered world.

Setting Precedent

In the summer of 1998, GCI retained a consulting firm to conduct a campaign assessment. The fund-raising capacity at that time was estimated at around $4 million. The GCI board needed a couple of months to discuss and embrace the venture. As their first major campaign and one of the first ever for a Latino-based agency, this was a decision that could affect more than GCI—it could set precedent for the Hispanic community.

Once the decision was made, architects rendered ideas and ideologies. executive director Cris Medina explained, "We knew what we needed to make this facility functional. The architects wanted to build something that made a statement about our cultural achievements. We were supportive of that picture, but every time we spoke with the architects, the price and the campaign goal increased. We finally came to a middle ground between the look and the function of the facility."

The initial estimate was $4.1 million. Eventually that campaign number rested at $4.9 million, although $5.1 million was ultimately raised. Renovations to the 6,000-square foot center, and an additional three-story, 18,000-square foot building connect form and function. "It's a building behind a building,"

Medina said. "They will be connected by a long walkway. It will look very nice."

The campaign process experienced heavy turnover in staffing. "We went through four development directors through the course of the campaign. One thing we do at GCI is to give young people a chance to learn and grow. The positive side was that all our development directors were personally familiar with the organization. They all came into the development director position knowing a lot about the mission of GCI. They moved on to other good jobs, but they will always remember GCI and appreciate our work," Medina said.

The lead gift came in August 1998 from the Hall Family and Hallmark Cards. The original gift of $675,000 was later upped to $1.1 million. Steering committee members were active in opening doors to potential donors. Said Medina, "I went to all the solicitations, but without an introduction from members of our steering committee, most of those calls would not have happened. I would tell people, 'If you can get me in there, I can present our case' and they did."

One volunteer, teaching ESL English class at GCI, turned out to be a real key to opening doors. This older gentleman, not in the best health, had quietly donated a decade of his retirement years to teaching English at GCI. "I worked for this man right after I graduated from college," Medina explained. "He had been the CEO of a manufacturing company for 20 years and now he was volunteering his time to GCI. It took some prodding, but I convinced him to be on the campaign steering committee."

The campaign also experienced its share of disappointments. A Kresge Foundation grant looked like a distinct possibility. The word was the Foundation was interested in funding Latino causes. Kresge, however, decided against a grant to GCI. It considered GCI gifts too heavily weighted by foundations and corporations over major gifts from individuals. The board donated $39,000 and the steering committee gave $20,000—not huge numbers to some, but they represented major sacrifices.

A Mabee challenge grant of $750,000 was a win, but not without an 11th hour wait. One week before the September 15th deadline to receive the challenge grant, GCI had not yet met the goal. "It was close," said Medina. "We barely made it, but William Dunn, Sr. came to bat for us with a big gift."

Supporting the Arts: Culinary and Cultural

Guadalupe Center had a very tight focus during its campaign and combined facilities expansion directly with program initiatives. Of the $5.1 million raised, $500,000 was targeted in support of two programs, culinary arts and cultural arts, each at $250,000. The balance of the campaign was in support of the facilities needed to house and showcase these educational initiatives. In the course of marketing the campaign, GCI was able to land a $2 million program grant from the U.S. Department of Labor in support of culinary arts education. Although the total dollars could not be counted in the campaign goal, it demonstrates how an integrated campaign—one that considers all revenue streams strategically—can grow an organization in a variety of ways.

The majority of GCI's programs, services, events, and activities are currently held in separate buildings: GCI Administration Building, Alta Vista Education Center, Casa Feliz Senior Center, Our Lady of Guadalupe Elementary School, Plaza de Ninos Preschool, Guadalupe Youth Center and Gymnasium, and Guadalupe Salud Center. The development of a culinary and cultural arts expansion to the current GCI Administrative Building creates training and employment opportunities and helps preserve the Latino heritage through the cultural arts.

The project will quadruple the size of the existing building—from 6,000 to 24,000 square feet—increasing the number of programs available and the number of individuals served. The culinary arts wing of the expansion will have two major components: a food preparation vocational training facility and a nonprofit catering service. These programs are essential in the Center's new initiative to create self-sustaining and revenue-generating programs. The program utilizes this area's designation as an Enhanced Enterprise Community (EEC) to further strengthen and increase services to the community. Kansas City (Kansas and Missouri) received $25 million in federal funds for economic development projects and an additional $2.4 million for social service and community-based programs. From this funding, GCI received a grant for the initial operations of the culinary arts program.

An additional goal is to construct a multipurpose facility for cultural and folkloric arts education programs, special events, and exhibits that exemplify the Latino culture. There will also be gallery space for Latino art and a theater for performing arts.

A Celebration of Success

"My mother's parents migrated to Kansas City in 1919, the same year the Guadalupe Center was established. She participated in fiestas and remembers Dorothy Gallager, the woman that built this place. After twenty years of service to the community, we are now empowered to give people an even greater opportunity to grow and develop," Medina said. "This campaign has increased our visibility. There is now not one major foundation in the Kansas City area that doesn't know we're here. We brought many people out to see the work we do. Most had never been here before the campaign. Now that it's over, I feel like the proud father of a new infant. People from the neighborhood call to me, 'Hey, good job.' Our most recent annual awards banquet, a black tie event held downtown, was the largest gathering ever—1,000 people came out. They knew we really had something to celebrate this year," added Medina.

"We interviewed a number of consultants before starting this campaign. We needed a consultant to teach us how to campaign for ourselves. I would tell our counsel that I wanted an 'A' for this class," said Medina. "He guided and had an ability to recognize our talents and shortcomings and give us advice accordingly. It's been a very good relationship. We were one of their first minority community organizations, so I believe the process was informative for them as well."

The consultant responded, "Cris Medina and his staff are among the most dedicated and persistent nonprofit managers I have ever known. Cris, in particular, set the pace and became increasingly tenacious, in the best sense, as the campaign moved forward. Despite setbacks during the campaign that included the turnover of four development directors and the death of the Center's business officer, Cris kept the leadership's spirits up. He wanted an 'A' for his first course in fund raising. I would give him an 'A+' because of his level of dedication."

From humble beginnings to a historic $5.1 million campaign, the Guadalupe Center, Inc. Culinary and Cultural Art Expansion showcases a proud heritage and a prosperous and productive future.

51

Growing Downtown
YWCA of Topeka

The YWCA of Topeka joined the growing YWCA move-
ment in 1887. Its current day mission "to create opportunities for women's
growth, leadership, and power in order to attain a common vision: peace, jus-
tice, freedom, and dignity for all people" was expressed even at the turn of the
century, with practical expressions of support—affordable residential rooms,
inexpensive meals, and a job referral service for young women.

By 1909, growth of the YWCA of Topeka led to the need for a building
large enough to house all the services provided by the organization. In 1911 the
first YWCA of Topeka was opened at 7th and VanBuren. The three-story house
included a swimming pool in the basement—the only location where women
could swim, in a time when men and women could not share swimming facilities.

Through the years the YWCA of Topeka adapted to the changing needs
of women and families. In the 1920s, with women entering more diverse jobs
and professions, the YWCA led the formation of groups such as the Business
Girl's League, the Young Matrons, the Negro Business and Professional Women's
Club, the Girl Reserves, and the Senoritas Club.

When the Depression hit in the 1930s, the organization provided a
soup kitchen for the community, a women's unemployment bureau, and services for families dislocated by economic loss. In 1953, a year prior to the Brown
vs. Board of Education decision, the YWCA of Topeka fully adopted integrated
policies and welcomed all members of the community into the YWCA family.

Decades of change created new challenges for women and the YWCA
programs adapted with the change. By the mid-'80s, childcare, health and well-

ness, and services to victims of domestic violence were now important YWCA programs. In 11 satellite locations around the city, the YWCA continued the mission it began over a century before.

Planning Decision

In 1996, the YWCA of Topeka Board of Directors adopted a more defined vision statement: "The YWCA of Topeka shall be the women's leadership center within the greater Shawnee County community with the financial, facility, and other resources necessary to support all approved programs that empower girls and women to achieve leadership positions within their homes, employment, and community."

Attaining the goal would require extensive renovations to its main site at West 12th Street (the organization had long outgrown its 7th Street beginnings). The 41,507-square foot building downtown was currently housing a childcare center, a teen pregnancy prevention area, domestic violence and sexual assault programs, health and fitness programs, and administrative offices. "In our experience, the YWCA of Topeka clearly has one of the most comprehensive series of women's programs of any group," offered a consultant for the group's downtown capital campaign.

As early as 1995, the Board and staff recognized a need to expand and renovate its building. Constructed in 1976, the 12th Street facility was due for some remodeling. Mechanical systems were inefficient, the roof needed attention, and office and meeting space was at a premium. Fulfilling the vision of becoming a "center" for services to women and families would require a capital campaign of significant proportions.

In the spring of 1997, the organization was approached by a retirement community and offered a gift of land. The reciprocal gift was that the YWCA agree to build a health and fitness center open to the community and accessible to the retirement residents. The proposal had potential for mutual merit, but the question at hand was whether the YWCA could stretch its mission beyond the downtown area and take on the responsibility of another facility.

A year was spent internally considering this possibility. After much discussion, a clear answer was still elusive. Said Kay Coles, YWCA of Topeka's executive director, "We really believed an external assessment was necessary to make this decision. After searching for a consultant to oversee this process, we retained a firm in the fall of 1998. The study was based on a premise that we would undertake a $5 million capital campaign for the new building in the southwest part of the city as well as remodel the downtown facility. The consultants conducted an assessment and reported back to the Board that there was not enough support to expand to the southwest. There was, however, strong support to expand and renovate downtown."

In November 1998 the Board voted to proceed with a campaign for $2.5 million, which included a $250,000 endowment. An impressive line-up of leadership offered a hint of the success this campaign could expect. "We were fortunate to recruit four of the top CEOs in the area, as well as the State Attorney General, Carla Stovall," Coles said.

"Then we had an important event occur in the summer of 1999. Security Benefit Group of Companies, one of the largest companies in Topeka, was building a new facility and interested in selling its existing one to the State of Kansas. I read an article about this in the newspaper back in February of '99. The article indicated that the State was not interested in buying Security Benefit's childcare building. The company had an interesting history with YWCA. Coincidentally, the city's first YWCA building had been razed to put in Security Benefit's parking lot. The company had supported YWCA and the CEO, Howard Fricke, was an honorary co-chair for the campaign steering committee. I called Howard and mentioned the article. I asked him if Security Benefit Group was interested in donating the childcare center to a worthy organization. 'Why?' he asked—well aware of my intentions—'Do you have a worthy organization in mind?'"

Rest is History

The rest is history for YWCA and Security Benefit Group. The company generously donated the freestanding childcare building to YWCA of Topeka (valued at $1 million with furnishings). With this gift, the steering committee recommended, and the Board agreed, in August to adjust the campaign goal up from $2.5 million to $3.5 million. This was a major milestone in the campaign and it greatly increased momentum for the remainder of the effort.

The donated building, located about six blocks from YWCA's downtown facility, put the campaign "on the map." By the fall of 1999, YWCA received Board member gifts, with 100 percent financial participation. "Our consultants laid out a strategic plan that involved grants, corporate gifts and a Kansas Community Service Income Tax Credit Grant, which we applied for in the summer of '99. From this, we received $300,000 of tax credits for cash gifts," said Coles.

Significant Gifts

Major corporations began giving toward the campaign at a fairly rapid clip. Impressive grant gifts also highlighted the YWCA campaign. In November 1999, Coles and a team of steering committee members traveled to the Mabee Foundation in Tulsa. Presenting the case for renovations to the downtown facility, YWCA was notified in January 2000 that the organization had received a $525,000 Mabee challenge grant.

In September of 2000, YWCA received a Kresge grant for $225,000. Many corporations that donated to the campaign at the leadership level ($25,000 and above) gave the largest gifts they had ever given in Topeka. AmVestors Financial, Inc. and Hallmark Cards each gave $150,000. Hallmark, with a plant in Topeka, pledged a gift to the YWCA campaign that doubled their previous high to any Topeka organization.

"Our steering committee really opened doors in the community. It is very unusual to get four highly visible CEOs on a steering committee. We knew this put us in good shape from the beginning. Also, YWCA has a long history in Topeka—and a good reputation for running quality programs and responding to community needs. One thing we realized over the course of the campaign was the YWCA had tremendous community support. You believe your programs are excellent and your work is important, but people are just too busy to spontaneously stop and show appreciation for what you do. The campaign created a public awareness of our work and provided a natural opportunity for the community to show its appreciation. The campaign was very energizing for our staff. We received positive and demonstrated feedback and support from the community through the campaign process," Coles said.

Additions and renovations to the downtown facility will come in three phases: 1) a 14,000-square foot Battered Women Task Force Center, and Health Arena, scheduled for April 2001; 2) 2,000-square feet area for the Girls to Girls program, as well as swimming pools and locker rooms, scheduled for December 2001; and 3) minor renovations to the new YWCA childcare academy acquired from Security Benefit Group of Companies, to be completed by June 2002.

Staff Leadership

"Kay Coles ran this campaign from start to finish. For someone who might not consider herself a fund raiser by nature or by experience, Kay did a masterful job of getting YWCA's story before the right people and making this campaign a real success," affirmed the campaign counsel.

"Actually, the consultants were our partners from the very beginning of this campaign. They helped us lay out the strategy and gave essential guidance on how to secure the gifts. If it had not been for their direct assistance and constant, relentless prodding—I mean encouragement—we would not have been as successful. It's pretty special in this community to receive $750,000 from out of state. This would not have occurred without the coaching (and prodding) we received," said Coles.

For over a century, YWCA of Topeka has been instrumental in the community—matching the needs of women and families with high-quality, accessible programs and support. With the additions and renovations provided through the Downtown Capital Campaign, YWCA is building a strong center of support for another century of service.

52

A Dream Come True

Exploration Place

The widow of visionary Walt Disney was asked to speak at Disney World's grand opening in Orlando, Fla. As she was introduced, the master of ceremonies turned to her and said effusively, "I just wish Walt could have seen this!" Mrs. Disney stood, moved to the microphone and answered emphatically, "He did."

Vision is the forerunner of anything great, and Wichita's new Exploration Place is the result of great vision on a grand scale. This does not diminish the enormity of effort in bringing the vision to pass. Still, without an ability to "see" the finished project a decade before the first shovelful of dirt was lifted from the banks of Wichita's Arkansas River (accent on Kansas, thank you very much), Exploration Place might have remained a good idea that came and went.

Creating the Dream

Instead, something very powerful occurred. People with vision and with the ability to make dreams come true, began dreaming together. Well-known Wichita establishments, the Omnisphere and the Wichita Children's Museum, toyed with the possibility of combining their passions to create a place where children (of all ages) could enjoy learning in a very "please touch" environment. Part science museum and part theme park, Exploration Place fulfills this dream by allowing visitors to ask questions and find the answers as they explore the center's many spacious exhibits and hands-on centers.

Before this dream came true, however, many individuals, corporations, and foundations concluded that it was time to imagine big things for Wichita. Everyone knew Wichita ruled the air through aircraft industry, but Exploration Place would demonstrate its entrepreneurial and philanthropic prowess on land.

In 1989, the Wichita City Council affirmed their interest in conjoining the Omnisphere and Wichita Children's Museum into a $12 million facility. A committee, chaired by Phillip S. Frick, was assigned to research the ambitious venture. After several years of study, the committee determined that a larger undertaking was not only feasible, but preferable. The increased 1993 estimate was now $40 million. Sedgwick County's Commission voiced its support with an initial pledge of $20 million. Then Velma Wallace, the widow of longtime Wichita aviation pioneer Dwane Wallace, endorsed the idea with a very generous pledge of $10 million. The dream was taking shape.

Momentum (as one could discover at Exploration Place) is motion equivalent to the product of a body's mass times its velocity. By 1995, the campaign to bring a massive learning center to downtown Wichita was picking up speed. The Wichita City Council agreed to spend $10 million for property, adjust a major boulevard, and donate 20 acres for the museum's use.

Can we Raise $62 Million?

Fund-raising counsel was retained to provide an assessment and ongoing fund-raising support. Said Phil Frick, "Our fund-raising goal was solidified after we received the final architectural plans and the building for Exploration Place was given equal weight with exhibits and programs. That number turned out to be $62 million."

The campaign goal included the cost of the building, improvements to the 20-acre site, exhibits, programs, staff costs, and an endowment. Through a creative plan, the City of Wichita provided a lease of property to the county. Sedgwick County, owners of the building, extended a long-term agreement with Exploration Place to house its exhibits and programs—a symbiotic arrangement that would benefit the owners and tenants, as well as neighboring businesses and the Wichita community.

Forward-thinking foundations, corporations, and individuals added their names and financial weight to the effort. In December 1993, John S. and James L. Knight Foundation pledged $250,000 toward the project. By 1996, gifts were becoming more frequent. Boeing Company contributed another $1.5 million in January of that year. Other gifts followed: Forrest C. Lattner Foundation donated $510,000 in April (eventually increased to $1 million), Wichita philanthropists Oliver and Betty Elliott gave $500,000 in October, and the Kansas Health Foundation closed out '96 with a pledge of $3.2 million (upped later to $5.2 million).

The next few years saw more support and additional gifts. In 1997, William T. Kemper Foundation gave $2 million in February toward the project. On May 31, 1997 the ground-breaking ceremony for Exploration Place signaled the beginning of an exciting new phase. In August, Mrs. Heber Beardmore donated $2 million in honor of her late husband and Raytheon Aircraft threw in its support with a gift of $2.5 million.

The next year, Koch Industries and Fred C. and Mary R. Koch Foundation gave a total of $1 million. Kansas Legislature approved a contribution of $1.5 million and Southwestern Bell donated $300,000 in the spring of '98. The descendants of Wichita aviation pioneers Walter and Olive Ann Beech gave nearly $1.5 million in the fall. Bloomfield Foundation closed out the year with a $1 million gift. Another million dollar gift came in from Cessna in the spring of 2000.

Staff Critical to the Dream

Dr. Al DeSena was hired from Pittsburgh, Pennsylvania in 1993 to serve as Exploration Place's president. "Moving from Pittsburgh and its wide base of corporate giving, I wondered to what extent this community could stretch to achieve a $62 million goal. There was actually significant support from many corporate and philanthropic sectors in Wichita. What was also impressive was how the campaign came together through the efforts of a relatively small staff. Much of that is due to the enormous effort of Phil Frick. Consequently, we were able to accomplish our goal without spending a lot of money. The percentage allocated to fund raising was probably less than most major campaigns. Our development staff was not large. Without question, the initial $30 million was great incentive, but there was still another $32 million to raise. Of course Phil Frick worked hard and steady from the beginning. I was the first paid staff member and we just have one director of development and one assistant. It is still amazing how much was achieved," said Dr. DeSena.

Gifts were reciprocated by either a "place" as an exhibition sponsor, or a "plaque" with name recognition. At least one Wichita business gave an initial gift to sponsor an exhibition, and then, as the building began its rise from alongside the river, they came back with a second gift for a naming opportunity. More mass. Greater velocity.

The Education of our Prospects

"I think the most important lesson we learned was that prospective donors want to be educated about the project. They want to know why the project is important to the community. This takes substantially more effort and time than is usually expected," stated Chairman Frick. "We have received extraordi-

211

nary gifts from dozens of individuals, corporations and foundations. Considering these gifts were solicited and obtained over an eight-year period, they were all instrumental in continuing the momentum and validating the importance of our project," he added. "Throughout the campaign, our consultant offered on-going expertise and I really doubt we could have achieved our goal without his help. His most important addition was probably the influence in the overall competency of the campaign," added President DeSena.

All of Wichita and environs have enjoyed a mutual pride in unveiling Exploration Place to the world. Featuring more than 98,000-square feet of indoor space, with fascinating, interactive exhibits, theaters and programs, Exploration Place is a Mecca for the imagination. The Center offers plenty to read and more to explore, but it is definitely not a "textbook" library or museum. No one will ask you to lower your voice or keep your hands to your sides. Rather, visitors are encouraged to get involved, ask questions, and try things out on their own.

Children visiting Exploration Place seem to catch on more quickly than the adults who walk slowly from display to display, glancing at the pictures and reading over the instructions. Kids, on the other hand, run right up and stick their hands into the tornado of vapor, crease their sheets of paper into airplanes and throw them across the room, push the buttons, play in the water, and follow the directions to explore.

A Conclusion that looks Forward

"There were," said Wichita mayor Bob Knight, "a lot of back-seat drivers: 'Don't get too bold. Don't dream these great, exciting dreams, because they could never be.'" The opening of Exploration Place in the spring of 2000 was literally a dream come true. What some cities would consider a flight of fancy, Wichitans saw as an opportunity. The idea of raising $62 million would exceed the scope of imagination for many, but like the dream makers of Exploration Place, great visionaries have always made life more interesting for the rest of life's explorers.

53

Creating a Classroom for Democracy

The Harry S. Truman Library Institute for National and International Affairs

"Harry Truman's greatest gift lay not in expression, but in decision—and in decision his courage and independence were exemplary. The list of his epoch-making decisions is extraordinary. Quite simply, Harry Truman changed the world."

Abba Eban
Former Israeli Ambassador to the U.S.
Truman Library, April 19, 1998.

In many ways, history becomes clearer the further away we stand. Bias and personal preference must move aside as time confirms what is true and enduring, and reveals what is ignoble and unstable. Such is the time-honored heritage and enduring power of the Truman legacy. Even Winston Churchill, a Truman contemporary not known for his high regard of many men beyond his statesman father and himself, was bold in his assessment of Harry S. Truman's stature and influence, "You, more than any other man, have saved Western civilization." (January 5, 1952).

For almost eight years, President Truman directed the United States through difficult days to new beginnings—the end of World War II, the establishment of the United Nations, the Truman Doctrine, the Marshall Plan, the desegregation of the Armed Forces, the recognition of Israel, the Korean conflict, the Berlin blockade and more. He is also remembered for his political prowess—his Whistlestop campaign, the day of the fair deal, his timeless values, decisiveness, and commitment to democracy. At home and abroad, Truman left a permanent impression of historic proportions.

Public and Private Support

The Truman Library Institute, Independence, Missouri, launched its $22.5 million campaign with a unique partnership between the public and private sectors. The Creating a Classroom for Democracy renovation project was initiated to support three fundamental concerns: pace-setting exhibits and educational spaces; outreach and public programs; and annual operations support.

On July 28, 2000, Missouri Governor Mel Carnahan announced a $2 million appropriation in state funding for the project. The money was given to support two new permanent exhibits as well as the Learning Center on Decision Making and Citizenship. (Governor Carnahan died tragically in a plane crash in October 2000.) Federal funding followed in August 2000 when Senator Kit Bond announced bipartisan support from the U.S. Congress for an $8 million appropriation to be used toward the physical renovation of the 43-year old building and to prepare it for expanded exhibitions and educational programs.

Renovations included: adjusting space on two floors for new permanent and temporary exhibit galleries; constructing rooms for the new Truman Library Learning Center; upgrading the museum lobby; constructing a new video theater; expanding the museum's gift shop; modernizing the auditorium; expanding public meeting rooms in the museum's east wing; upgrading the museum's security system and environmental controls; and providing accessibility for persons with disabilities.

For the last forty years, the Truman Library has been enjoyed by more than 8 million visitors. Over 10,000 on-site researchers have used the Truman Library archives, which house Truman's presidential papers and 400 other unique collections. Hundreds of thousands of virtual visitors are now offered information via the internet. Growing interest in the conflicts and resolutions of the World War II era have increased the demand for the Truman Library programming and services.

Campaign Goal Established

The $22.5 million campaign, conducted with counsel, encompassed 39,000-square feet of renovations and added 4,500-square feet of new construction. The original goal was allocated for the three major areas of emphasis: $9.38 million for the design, fabrication, and installation of the pace-setting exhibits and educational spaces; $5.12 million for expanded outreach and public programs; five years of operating new educational programs; and $8 million for repair and upgrades to the existing building.

"True leadership is the lesson taught in this Library that President Truman conceived as a classroom of democracy—and which, 40 years after it first opened—is undergoing a fresh renewal and revitalization to reflect both the challenges and the opportunities of a new century," observed President Gerald R. Ford on May 8, 1998.

Making Use of Your Ground Breaking

In May 2000, forty-five years to the day that Harry S. Truman broke ground for the Truman Library, construction for the Creating a Classroom for Democracy project was publicly announced. An important feature of the Library expansion and renovations is the White House Decision Center (WHDC). This exciting and interactive educational program offers 60 high school students per day an opportunity to step back in time and act as key policy advisors to the president on a specific issue such as the Berlin Airlift, desegregation of the Armed Services, the Korean stage of conflict, and other challenges of the Truman era. Students take the roles of the secretary of state, chairman of the joint chiefs, and other key officials involved in the Korean situation. After much discussion and debate, taking place in seven meeting rooms resembling the West Wing of the White House, the students ultimately reach a presidential decision on the day's issue. Students participate in research and analysis before defending their positions—bringing the classroom to life and exposing another generation to the real challenges of leadership and decision making.

Speaking at the May ceremony, the oldest grandson of President Truman, Clifton Truman Daniel, provided the keynote address. "Beyond the Library there is a beautiful town here that supports the Library," said Daniel. Support for the campaign came from many corporations and individuals. Gifts of a million dollars or more were received from the Hall Family Foundation, the Sosland Foundation, James B. Nutter and family, as well as one anonymous donor.

Staff Leadership Directed the Project

"Private funding will help support all areas of the Classroom for Democracy," explained Larry Hackman, Executive Director for The Truman Library Institute during the campaign.

"It was Larry's vision and connection to the Kansas City community that gave this campaign momentum. While he may not have favored fund raising over his other duties, Larry's sincerity and commitment to the Library and to the Classroom for Democracy gave him tremendous credibility and influence in the philanthropic community. The Library's Director of Development, Jeffrey Byrne, was terrific at focusing the campaign and operating it daily," said the campaign's counsel.

The Library's renovated areas will open in phases beginning in February 2001 with the premiere of Presidential Portraits, a traveling exhibition from the Smithsonian Institute's National Portrait Gallery, in the Library's new changing exhibitions gallery. The Presidential Galleries will focus on the major policies, decisions and events of the Truman Administration and offer an overview of the Truman legacy. The Life and Times Galleries will showcase artifacts that illustrate the story of Truman's personal life.

Wild About Connecting with the Community

The Truman Library Institute's second annual gala Wild About Harry raised $155,000 to benefit Truman Library public programs. Hackman announced at this April 2000 event that the campaign had surpassed its original goal of $22.5 million, at that time raising $23.7 million in cash and firm pledges, plus $1.6 million in deferred gifts.

Hackman offered, "The best part of the campaign has been the relationships that we have begun to develop with individuals and organizations here in Kansas City. Indeed, of the private gifts and pledges, more than 90 percent has come from the Kansas City area."

Donations of $5,000 and above are recognized on a donor wall in the Truman Library's lobby. All donations are acknowledged in a book of donors (similar to the one created for donors of the original Library Building Fund in 1957) kept permanently at the museum.

Said Hackman, "We are deeply grateful to business and community leaders in Kansas City for their early support of this fund-raising campaign. It is clear they identify strongly with the Truman Library's vision for the future. These contributions will help fulfill the hope that this presidential library will be a classroom for democracy for all ages."

54

Chanute Depot Restoration Campaign
Chanute Public Library and the Martin and Osa Johnson Safari Museum

It did not happen by accident or through luck. Raising $2 million in a town the size of Chanute, Kansas (population: 9,500) took hard work, advanced planning and professional fund-raising advice. The fact that it could be done at all, surprised most of its citizens. The fact that it was accomplished in less than two years—from the announcement of the project in mid-April 1990 to the final pledge that put it over the top in January 1992—provided immense satisfaction.

The campaign had a head start with a pledge from local businessman Larry Hudson. His family foundation committed $500,000 to get the Chanute Depot Restoration Project started. The original goal was $1.5 million. The money would be used to restore the old Santa Fe Depot into new homes for The Chanute Public Library and the Martin and Osa Johnson Safari Museum.

Setting Goals

Mike Mitchell, president of Nu-Way Industries, a manufacturer of recreational vehicles and campers, was asked to head the campaign. Mitchell agreed to come onboard as campaign chairman in late July 1990. He and Hudson decided on an aggressive approach to fund raising. They recommended pushing the goal to $1.75 million.

217

Hudson, motivated by the enthusiasm of the effort, agreed to match all funds between the original goal of $1.5 million and $1.75 million—increasing the final goal to $2 million.

A steering committee was formed with seven persons—three each, selected from both the library and museum, and one representative from the city. (The depot was owned by the city.) A fund raising consulting firm was retained as campaign counsel in early July 1990.

Making a Case for Chanute

The committee began writing a campaign plan and case statement for the renovation of the depot. It then incorporated the history of the Santa Fe Railroad Company—since the railroad played an important role in the early life of Chanute.

Historians for these three entities were asked to submit histories, provide descriptions of their needs, show how their needs would be met through the restoration project and demonstrate the economic advantages to Chanute.

Next, the committee planned a timetable, established how much money needed to be raise, determined where the money would come from and what kinds of gifts would be accepted. At the same time, they designed a public relations plan to support the fund raising process.

Refining a "final" case statement and campaign plan was no easy task. However, goodwill and determination prevailed, and by the first meeting in September 1990, all campaign documents were finalized and approved.

Good Prospecting

Next, the committee identified prospective donors. Each committee member submitted as many names as possible, with many duplicates ending up on the cutting room floor. As they continued the arduous process, the list was refined to include 300 potential donors. They followed the campaign counsel's "rule of thumb": three names for each gift sought.

In a small town the size of Chanute, where everyone knows everyone, traditional prospect research did not seem necessary. Donor interests, how they spend their money, etc., were already fairly well known.

The initial timetable was short for a project of this size. The goal was to complete the campaign a year from the announcement. The committee identified prospects and developed a visual presentation to nurture interest in the project. They knew, however, that before they could solicit money, they would need to put their own money on the line.

218

Chart of Giving

Committee members developed a campaign prospectus, which was personally delivered to prospective donors.

The first contacts were made in October 1990, with each member of the Steering Committee selecting a number of the prospects to call upon. A campaign chart of giving identified the needs as follows:

CHART OF GIFTS

Gift Number	Size of Gifts	Total Gifts
1(gift of)	$500,000	$500,000
1	200,000	700,000
3	100,000	1,000,000
6	50,000	1,300,000
8	25,000	1,500,000
10	10,000	1,600,000
20	5,000	1,700,000
35	1,000	1,735,000
Other	Many	$1,750,000

Once they raised $175,000, the $250,000 challenge gift would take the campaign to $2 million.

When raising funds, most of the support comes from very few donors and less support comes from a great many donors. Of $1.74 million raised, 18 contributors donated $25,000 or more, which made up about 87 percent. Of the top 18 contributors, seven were individuals or families, seven were local businesses and four were national or regional corporations and foundations. Of the 99 other contributions—those between $1,000 and $20,000—73 were from individuals, 24 from local businesses and two from local organizations. Individual or team solicitations were made for requests of $25,000 and more.

Going Public

With the major solicitations nearly completed in March 1991, the committee began to market the "Buy-a-Shelf Campaign." Shelves were sold for $500 and brought in 72 donations for a total of $36,000.

The public campaign began on Depot Day in May. The event was filled with festivities, including depot tours (pre-renovation), train rides, a book sale, "Harvey Girl" hostesses, and skits (turn-of-the-century vignettes by the local community theater group). There was an auction, homemade and concession food, antique cars, a fun run, and many other events. In total, Depot Day contributed another $34,000 to the overall campaign, including several large contributions of $5,000 and $1,000. The momentum was kept up throughout the summer of 1991.

The steering committee was small—10 in all. The Library and Museum boards selected committee members—not particularly for their abilities to be major donors. Therefore, not all committee members felt comfortable or qualified to solicit major contributions. Mr. and Mrs. Mike Mitchell, campaign co-chairs, provided one of the first major gifts and became two of the most influential solicitors.

A Public/Private Partnership

The city's involvement in the campaign was commendable. It was truly a public/private partnership. The city was able and willing to provide the up-front financing so that the campaign could accept donations over a five-year pledge period. In addition, the city provided the land and purchased the depot from Santa Fe.

As time progressed, everyone seemed to want to get in on the act. The campaign treasurer was a local banker whose bank provided the bookkeeping for money and pledges before turning the funds over to the city. This provided accountability on the status of funds.

There was also tremendous support from the local newspaper. The restoration was front-page news throughout most of the campaign—with articles and many pictures to help get the story across.

Completing the Goal

The campaign reached $1 million by November 1990. By February 1991, it was at $1.25 million. Then, in mid-April, things slumped—nothing but rejections. They were stalled at $1.33 million and committee members became discouraged.

The campaign goal was abruptly lowered to $1.62 million, reducing the matching grant and decreasing the total goal to $1.75 million.

The campaign continued and by the end of May 1991, they had surpassed $1.5 million. Another $25,000 in local business donations a month later brought us to $1.6 million. By late August, they were only $140,500 away from reaching $1.75 million. With interest in the campaign picking up, donations began to pour in—many between $100 to $500—with some larger donations as well. By October 1991, they needed only $127,000.

This was the hardest point in the campaign. Contributions of major gifts were still being sought, but things seemed to be reaching a plateau. Committee members were getting tired and frustrated. The end was in sight, but still not within reach.

Another Christmas holiday came and went and they still had not quite reached the goal. On January 3, 1992, the campaign director and Mike Mitchell decided to ask Larry Hudson if he would continue matching gifts until January 15. At that time, they were only $30,000 short. Hudson agreed, and in a frenzy of last minute negotiations, another business finally produced the gift that put the campaign over the top.

How was success achieved? Leadership, persistence and a sincere belief in the project. Committee members saw the vision of what the project would mean to Chanute and shared that vision with the citizens and business leaders of the town.

They were determined. They knew the money was there and they just did not quit short of the intended goal! They all believed that the project was in the best interest of Chanute. The job was to educate others and offer them an opportunity to give to the project.

55

Preserving the Past—
Preparing for the Future
Youth and Shelter Services

Builders and architects acknowledge that starting from scratch is easier than renovating an existing structure. Easier, but not necessarily better. The imagination and ingenuity it took to resurrect the long-vacant Ames Municipal Building was not only an investment in bricks and mortar, but also a metaphor for the work of its new owner, Youth and Shelter Services, Inc. of Ames, Iowa.

In its first 20 years, YSS helped restore and preserve the lives of more than 20,000 troubled young people by offering residential treatment programs, counseling, and assistance with family foster care and adoption. In addition, over 100,000 children, students, and parents have benefited from YSS's comprehensive prevention and education programs. The capital campaign, "Preserving the Past—Preparing for the Future," began with the dual goals of bringing many YSS programs to one central location, and strengthening the YSS Foundation endowment.

The renovated building pulled together programs such as: Pathways and Young Parents Center, Family House Counseling Center, Volunteer Programs, Child Safety/Parenting Education, Family Foster Care, Independent Living Programs, Delinquency and Violence Prevention, Substance Abuse Prevention and Education, and Administrative Support Services.

Historic Preservation

The municipal building sat empty for about five years after the previous owner, the city of Ames, moved its offices to another location. Youth and Shelter Services offered to buy the 17,500-square-foot building from the city for five hundred dollars and remodel and expand it to suit YSS's needs. The agency promised to maintain the historic exterior and asked the city to make parking available near the building. In 1995, the Ames City Council agreed on both counts—price and parking.

George Belitsos, YSS's founder and its only executive director had a vision for the old building, that could not be dimmed by accumulated dust, dank smelling rooms, or the $2 million needed to renovate and fill the empty facility. The building was slated for demolition. It had served as City Hall from 1915 until the City offices were moved in 1991.

"We had engineers inspect the building and they found it to be structurally sound. In fact, it was the first building west of the Mississippi River built with reinforced steel. We approached the opportunity from the historic value of the building and the architects made renovations in keeping with the building's classic American Revival architectural style," said Belitsos. Like many of the clients YSS serves, the building was rescued from difficult circumstances and given a second chance.

With its unique choice of location, (youth services are rarely housed in historically preserved buildings), YSS stepped away from the crowd and earned, in its bold venture, a new place of visibility in the community.

YSS selected local residents to serve on a Historic Preservation Committee to ensure that renovations of the exterior took into account the significance of the building. The architects and contractor took great care in restoration and came in under budget on the remodeling. The building, now listed in the National Register of Historic Places, retains the structure's overall integrity in its classic American Revival architectural style. Accessibility was what YSS needed—a centralized location, set in the heart of downtown Ames. History was a bonus; visibility was a by-product of both.

Taking an Assessment

An assessment conducted at the beginning of 1995, and presented in March 1995, set the campaign goal at $2 million for capital needs and $500,000 for endowment. The silent phase of the campaign started right away. The lead gift was announced fairly early in the campaign, strategically before the City sold the five hundred dollar building to Youth and Shelter Services.

It was a wonderful lead gift. A board member had a relationship with a long-time Iowa philanthropist. He was interviewed as part of the assessment and asked in June for a gift. The philanthropist was very interested in the work of YSS and especially taken with the idea of saving the old city hall. His $500,000 gift not only gave the campaign momentum, but also provided a new name for an old building. The "Preserving the Past—Preparing for the Future" campaign forever changed the historic Ames Municipal Building to the Richard O. Jacobson Youth and Family Center.

This relationship opened the door for a challenge from the Variety Club of Iowa. The match was a 3 to 1 gift. YSS would raise $1.2 million to receive Variety Club's $400,000 gift, all for capital costs. To raise endowment, YSS initiated an integrated capital and endowment campaign piece. The bulk of that goal was met through planned gifts, wills, insurance, bequests, and so on. Donors had to document gifts as endowment, but when it came time for recognition, capital and endowment gifts were honored equally and identically. The capstone donor was unexpected. The family, new to the Ames community, was introduced to YSS by an agency volunteer.

Renovations on the building started early in 1996. Once YSS secured it from the City, an inspiration turned almost magical. Executive Director Belitsos already had plans to place a time capsule into the building, to be opened by a future generation. In an uncanny twist of past and present, a time capsule from a previous generation was discovered in the wall of the old building.

A Time Capsule from the Past

After 81 years, the contents of the time capsule were removed as part of Iowa's 150th birthday celebration. The capsule could not be dislodged from the wall, so on January 24, 1996, items were removed piece by piece—to the delight of attendees—and the contents turned over to Iowa State University's Parks Library Conservator for cleaning and preservation. The items are now on display at the Ames Public Library.

A new time capsule was filled using ideas from a Sesquicentennial Time Capsule Contest in cooperation with YSS and the Story County Sesquicentennial Commission. Story County youth contributed suggestions for a new time capsule, placed in the remodeled building, to be opened on Iowa's 300th birthday in the year 2146.

YSS moved into the renovated building in April 1997. Outside the main entrance, donor bricks, honoring a donor's family and the date of their arrival in Ames, were engraved and set into the Family History Plaza. Again, the past meets the future, as new generations walk along the Family History Plaza and remember the connection.

YSS raised $ 2.78 million toward its capital and endowment campaign, exceeding the $2.5 million goal on the capital side. The actual pledge goal was met within nine months of the public announcement in December 1996—bringing the capstone in September 1997.

Greater Visibility

"The building lent itself to remodeling," said Belitsos. "The result was a pleasure for YSS staff and clients. The renovation and campaign brought us greater visibility in the community. Our annual campaigns have gone up since then, due to the recognition YSS received from this successful capital campaign. My advice to other nonprofits would be to think big. Have a vision that people can quickly identify and support. The more imaginative, the more visible, the more money you will raise. Don't be afraid to combine things that don't normally get combined—historic preservation and youth, for example."

The new Richard O. Jacobson Youth and Family Center makes services more accessible to central Iowa clients, increases space for individual and family counseling, redirects some current expenses to human needs, enhances productivity, provides handicapped accessibility, and promotes collaboration between staff and volunteers.

In restoring the Ames Municipal building, YSS exemplified the nature of philanthropy. The time and resources they invested in the building have come back to them in many ways. As philanthropist and YSS lead donor Richard Jacobson put it, in his speech at the 18th Annual Meeting of Youth and Shelter Services on May 18, 1994, "People often ask me why I continue to work and continue to make deals, when I could retire. The answer is easy—so that I can give more money and effort away to worthy causes. Giving is living because in giving, our lives are made better in every conceivable way. When we give to others—when we share our time, talent, and money—we do not end up with less in our accounts, but more."

About the Editor

Bob Hartsook is chairman and CEO of Hartsook Companies, Inc., which owns Hartsook and Associates and Essential Philanthropic Services. The company partners with ASR Philanthropic Publishing in its efforts to provide quality philanthropic information to the fund-raising community.

From the role of chief development officer of three universities and colleges, Bob moved to establishing the company in 1987. Now having been involved in over 500 campaigns across the country—regularly doing business in 25 states and maintaining a client list of more than 100 organizations—his firms have raised billions of dollars, satisfying organizational demands.

Bob holds a doctor of education and juris doctor, in addition to his masters in counseling and economic baccalaureate. He lives on Wrightsville Beach, N.C., with his son, Austin.

You may contact Dr. Hartsook at:

Dr. Robert F. Hartsook, Chairman and CEO
Hartsook and Associates
1501 Castle Rock
Wichita, KS 67230
Telephone: 316.733.7100
Facsimile: 316.733.7103
E-mail: bob@hartsookcompanies.com
Web Site: hartsookcompanies.com

ASR Philanthropic Publishing

ASR Philanthropic Publishing serves the fund-raising and philanthropic community with a variety of publications designed to inform and educate, as well as stimulate thought and discussion by professionals throughout the United States.

ASR publications include newsletters, books, and monographs, as well as audio and video products. In addition, ASR's Reference Collection monographs and books may be purchased in small or large quantities. Discounts apply to large-quantity orders. For large-quantity monograph orders, ASR can imprint your organization's logo or trademark on each copy. ASR customizes and binds collections of monographs that meet your organization's reference needs.

ASR Philanthropic Publishing has an active custom-publishing division that creates books, newsletters, brochures and other print material for use by fund-raising and philanthropic organizations. The firm is available to consult on your organization's specific needs.

To order or receive information about any of ASR's publications or programs please contact:

ASR Philanthropic Publishing
P.O. Box 782648
Wichita, Kansas 67278
Telephone: 316.733.7470
Facsimile: 316.733.7103
E-mail: info@asrpublishing.com
Web Site: www.ASRpublishing.com

Resources

Authors: The following individuals have contributed to this book.

Hart, Franci, *Director of Annual Support, Oklahoma City University*

Hartsook, JD, EdD, Robert F., *Chairman and CEO, Hartsook and Associates, Inc.*

Hawks, Lynn, *Senior Consultant, Hartsook and Associates, Inc.*

Kensett, Lee, *Campaign Chair, Chanute Depot Restoration Project*

Kresse, Jean, *Vice President, Hartsook and Associates, Inc.*

McAfee, Melinda, *Senior Consultant, Hartsook and Associates, Inc.*

Murphy, Norma R., *Vice President of Development, Cerebral Palsy Research Foundation of Kansas*

Rhoades, Denise D., *Freelance Writer*

Schneweis, Susan, *Senior Consultant, Hartsook and Associates, Inc.*

Staley, PhD, R. Eric, *Vice Chairman and Executive Vice President, Hartsook and Associates, Inc.*

Stevenson, Scott, *President, Stevenson Consultants, Inc.*

Swanson, Robert G., *President, Hartsook and Associates, Inc.*

Vine, Ronald A., *Consultant, Hartsook and Associates, Inc.*

Sources: The following individuals were willing to share their stories and strategies with the various authors. We appreciate their cooperation.

Bailey, Pat, *Board of Directors and Campaign Co-Chairman*
YWCA of Tulsa

Belitsos, George, *Executive Director*
Youth and Shelter Services, Inc.

Blackwelder, Murray, *Vice President of External Affairs*
Iowa State University

Chandler, John R. (Rusty), *Special Assistant to the Headmaster*
The Hotchkiss School

Coles, Kay, *Executive Director*
YWCA of Topeka

Cooper, Carla M., *Senior Vice President for Health Care Philanthropy*
St. Luke's Episcopal Hospital

DeSena, Dr. Al, *President*
Exploration Place

Frick, Phil, *Board of Directors Chairman and Campaign Chairman*
Exploration Place

Hackman, Larry, *Executive Director*
The Harry S. Truman Library Institute for
National and International Affairs

Helm, Peyton R., *Vice President for Development & Alumni Relations*
Colby College

Holland, Ned, *President*
Truman Medical Center Charitable Foundation

Jischke, Martin, *President*
Iowa State University

Litzler, Mark E., *Executive Director*
Truman Medical Center Charitable Foundation

McLaughlin, James, *Director of Development*
Botsford General Hospital

Meckfessel, Mary Ann, *Campaign Co-Chair*
YWCA of Tulsa

Medina, Cris, *Executive Director*
Guadalupe Center, Inc.

Merrill, Kay E., *Director of Development*
Boys & Girls Clubs of the Lowcountry, Inc.

Mitchell, Thomas, *President*
Iowa State University Foundation

Morgan, Karen, *Executive Director*
Girl Scout Council of the Ozark Area

Page, Kathleen, *Past President Board of Directors*
YWCA of Tulsa

Patton, Sara, *Vice President for Development*
The College of Wooster

Reppe, Dixie, *Executive Director*
YWCA of Tulsa

Schmidt, Rebecca, *Director of Stewardship*
The College of Wooster

Szuch, Patricia E., *Director of Capital Giving*
Ball State University

Vickerman, Larry, *Director*
Dyck Arboretum of the Plains

Vogel, Susan, *Manager*
Anne Arundel Medical Center

Walls, Karel, *Director of Development*
The Art Institute of Boston

Wood, Bonnie, *Director of Development*
Botsford General Hospital

ASR Philanthropic Publishing's Resource Reference Collection

ASR's Reference Collection addresses the important topics in fund raising and philanthropic management. Written by leading experts, these to-the-point publications are essential tools for fund raisers who excel. Following is a current list of available Reference Collection Monographs.

Annual Giving
#01-001	It's Worth a $5 Million Endowment
#01-002	Insuring the Annual Fund Program of Non-Profit Organizations. Announcing: The Forward Fund

Capital Campaigns
#02-001	10 Impediments to Campaign Success
#02-002	Why You Don't Need the 800-Pound Gorilla
#02-003	Stick to the Basics
#02-004	What to Do When The Campaign Is Over
#02-005	Identifying the Significant Gift Opportunity
#02-006	The Sizzle Factor
#02-007	30 Commandments for Successful Fund Raising
#02-009	Campaign For Dignity: Cerebral Palsy Research Foundation
#02-010	The Secret of Campaign Success: How Kansas Special Olympics Raised $1.35 Million
#02-011	Great Empires Aren't Built in a Day: Magic Empire Council of Girl Scouts

Planned Giving

Prospect Research

Recognition

Solicitation

Cultivation

Board Development

Volunteers

Major Gifts

To order a monograph contact:

ASR Philanthropic Publishing
P.O. Box 782648
Wichita, Kansas 67278
Telephone: 316.733.7470
Facsimile: 316.733.7103
E-mail: info@asrpublishing.com
Web Site: www.ASRpublishing.com

☐ **YES!** Send me the next two monthly issues of *Successful Fund Raising* free. If I choose not to subscribe, I will return your invoice marked "cancel" and owe nothing. If I decide to subscribe, I will pay the invoice amount of $99 — a savings of $21 off the regular price — for a one-year (12 issues) subscription.

Three easy ways to get your FREE 2-month trial subscription today!

☞ this postage-paid card

✈ to order: 712-239-3010

FAX: 712-239-2166

Name _____

Title _____

Organization _____

Address _____

City _____

State (Province) _____

Zip (Postal Code) _____

Daytime Phone (_____) _____

E-mail _____

To learn more about all our newsletters — *Successful Fund Raising*, *The Major Gifts Report* and *The Volunteer Managment Report* — visit our web site at: www.stevensoninc.com

HARTSOOK AND ASSOCIATES
ESSENTIAL PHILANTHROPIC SERVICES

☐ *Please contact me about how my nonprofit can improve its fund raising.*

Send me information on the following:

☐ *An integrated campaign*

☐ *An endowment campaign*

☐ *A capital campaign*

☐ *The creation of a deferred giving program*

☐ *A development operation evaluation*

☐ *Improving annual fund results*

☐ *Board and volunteer training related to fund raising*

☐ *A training/mentoring program for staff*

☐ *Other* _____

_____

NAME _____ TITLE _____

ORGANIZATION _____

ADDRESS _____ PHONE _____

CITY _____ STATE _____ ZIP _____ FAX _____

CALL (316) 733-7100

BUSINESS REPLY MAIL

FIRST CLASS MAIL   PERMIT NO. 284   SIOUX CITY, IA

POSTAGE WILL BE PAID BY ADDRESSEE

SUCCESSFUL
F UND RAISING

STEVENSON CONSULTANTS, INC.
P.O. BOX 4528
SIOUX CITY, IOWA 51104

BUSINESS REPLY MAIL

FIRST CLASS MAIL   PERMIT NO. 5112   WICHITA, KS

POSTAGE WILL BE PAID BY ADDRESSEE

HARTSOOK AND ASSOCIATES
PO BOX 782890
WICHITA KS 67278-9670